A Piece O' Cake

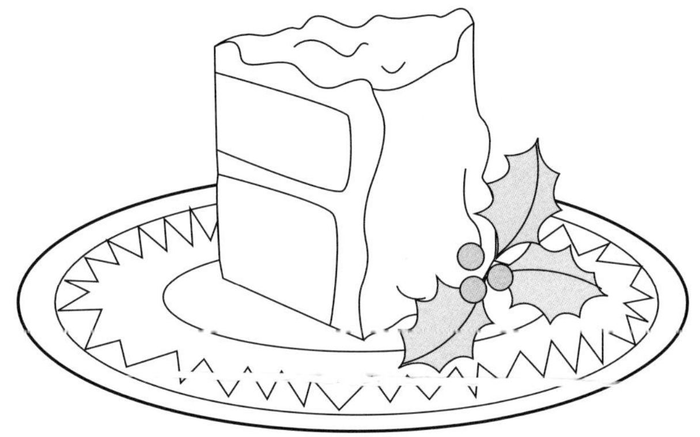

Christmas!

Linda Jenkins & Becky Goldsmith

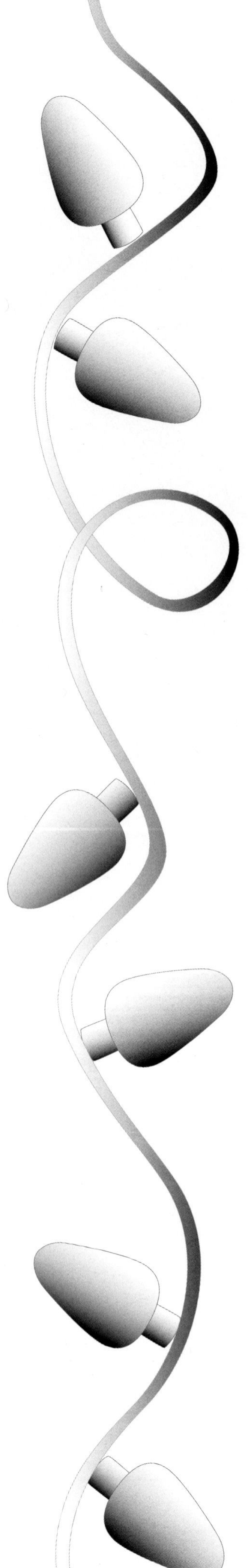

Acknowledgments

Thank <u>you</u> for supporting us! Your encouragement keeps us going (even on those days we'd rather take a nap!). We hope you enjoy this newest book.

We thank Billi Lackey, our office manager, for keeping us on track. If you call the office, you'll probably talk to Billi. We're betting you'll enjoy the conversation.

We thank Irwin Bear and P&B Textiles for their generous support. We used P&B fabric, including our collections Tulips in the Park and Frostings, for most of the projects in this book.

Last but by no means least we thank our husbands, Paul Jenkins and Steve Goldsmith, for supporting us in all we do.

Credits

Copy Editor ....Steve Goldsmith
Technical Editor...Linda Jenkins
Photography ....Chris Marona
Illustrations ....Becky Goldsmith
Quilts ....Linda Jenkins & Becky Goldsmith

Resources

Fairfield Processing Corp. (Soft Touch Batting)
Kunin Felt

A Piece O' Cake Christmas
ISBN 0-9674393-2-9
© 2000 by Linda Jenkins & Becky Goldsmith
Piece O' Cake Designs, Inc.
301 Handicap Avenue
Pagosa Springs, CO 81147
www.pieceocake.com

Introduction

We love the Christmas season. Everybody is bustling about, and yet we find the time for family and friends. It's a time of year when we dress up ourselves and our houses for the holidays. Quilts, with their warmth and beauty, are the perfect centerpiece for any room.

We have designed three new Christmas quilts for this book: 1950's Santa Claus, The Christmas Trees, and Reindeer Playground. Additionally, there are fast projects that you can make for yourself – or for a very lucky friend.

In designing the quilts for this book, we thought back to the Christmases that we remembered from the Fifties. Our Santa is jolly and round – with a distinctive, happy face. The reindeer have a spirited sleekness that is also reminiscent of the Fifties. The decorated Christmas Trees are just plain cute!

We hope you enjoy making these quilts and projects. We know that many of you are too strapped for time to hand applique every-thing in this book – so we have provided tips for those of you who want to fuse the applique. No matter what applique technique you use, we hope you enjoy these projects. We wish you Merry Christmas for many years to come.

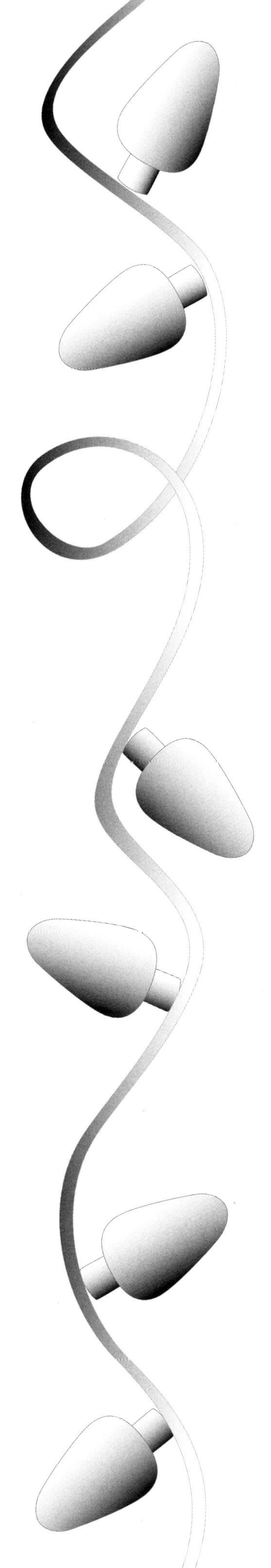

When Billi saw this spot, she said that we should have had our pictures taken with Santa hats on. What a good idea! Unfortunately, we're in different states and this book has to go to press. So, pretend this is a photo of us in cute red outfits (with matching shoes!).

Ho! Ho! Ho! Merry Christmas!

Table of Contents

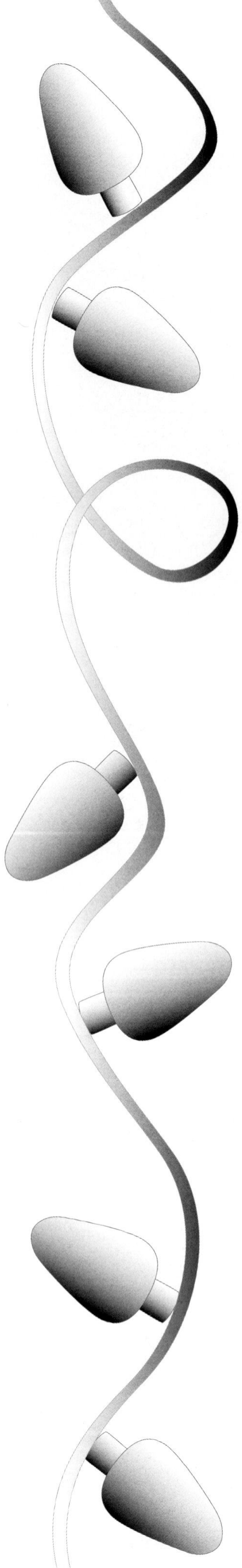

Basic Supplies

FABRIC. All of the fabrics used in the quilts in this book are 100% cotton unless otherwise stated. We pre-wash our fabric before using it. This is a good way to test for colorfastness. If the fabric is going to shrink, it does so before it's sewn into the quilt. And, the fabric smells and feels better if it is pre-washed.

We used polyester felt for the Christmas stockings and tree skirt. We did not pre-wash the felt. If you fuse felt appliques, test a scrap first. If your iron is too hot the felt can melt.

SCISSORS. Embroidery size scissors for both paper and fabric. Small scissors are better for intricate cutting.

NEEDLES. We like both sharps and straw needles for hand applique.

THREAD. Use cotton thread with cotton fabric. We prefer DMC 100% cotton 50 wt. machine embroidery thread for our hand applique. It says "broder machine" on the spool. This is also great thread for machine quilting.

PENCILS. Use either a white chalk pencil or a mechanical pencil when drawing around templates onto the fabric.

1/2" SEQUIN PINS. To pin your applique in place.

MARKER. An ultra fine point Sharpie® marker works best on the upholstery vinyl.

GEL PENS. For the Santa faces.

CLEAR UPHOLSTERY VINYL. 60" wide vinyl used to make a positioning overlay. You can usually find it in stores that carry upholstery fabric.

CLEAR SELF-LAMINATING SHEETS. Used to make templates, you can find them at most office supply stores and sometimes at warehouse markets.

SANDPAPER BOARD. Lay your fabric on the sandpaper side of the board, then lay your template on the fabric and trace. You'll love the way the sandpaper holds the fabric in place.

BATTING. We prefer cotton batting. Our favorite is Fairfield's Soft Touch 100% Cotton Batt.

THE APPLIQUE HANDBOOK. Refer to this book by Piece O' Cake Designs for detailed information on needleturn hand applique.

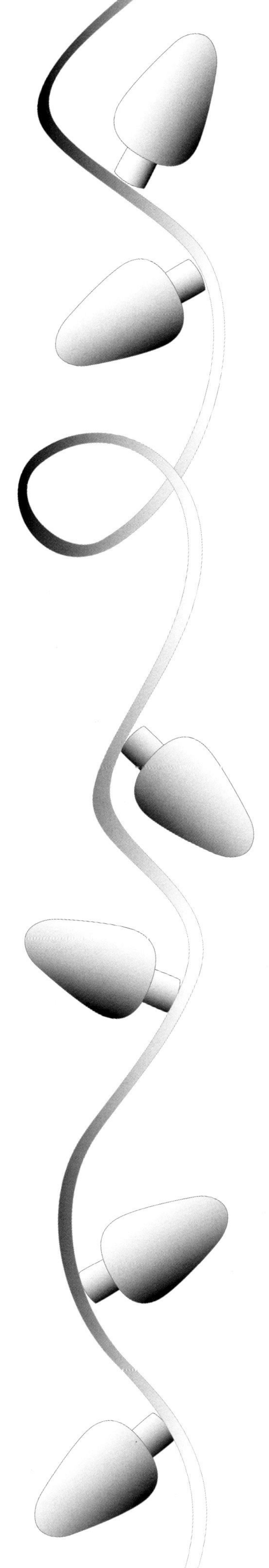

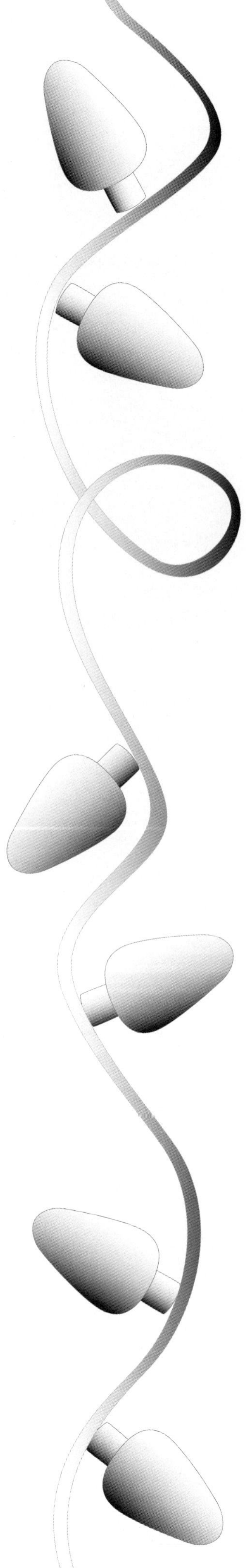

General Applique Instructions

Preparing Backgrounds for Applique

Always cut your background fabric larger than the size it will be when it is pieced into the quilt. The outer edges of your block can stretch and fray when you handle it while stitching. Your applique can shift during stitching and can cause your block to shrink slightly. For these reasons it is best to add 1" to all sides of your backgrounds when you cut them out.

Press each background block in half vertically and horizontally. This establishes a center grid in your background that will line up with the center grid on your positioning overlay. Once your applique is complete, press each block and carefully trim it to size. Always make sure that your design is properly aligned with your ruler before you cut off the excess fabric.

Positioning Overlay

The positioning overlay is used to place each applique piece accurately on the block. It is easy to make and use, and it makes your projects very portable. Cut a piece of clear upholstery vinyl, with its tissue paper lining, to the finished size of each block. Set the tissue paper aside until you are ready to fold or store your overlay.

Make a copy of the patterns in this book to work from. Where a pattern is in two pieces, tape them together. Tape a copy of a pattern onto the table in front of you. Tape the upholstery vinyl over it. Using a ruler and an ultra fine point Sharpie® marker, draw a line on the vinyl over the horizontal and vertical center lines on your pattern.

Trace the pattern accurately on the vinyl. The numbers on the pattern indicate stitching sequence. Include these numbers on your overlay.

To use the overlay, lay your background right side up on your work surface. Place the overlay over it, also right side up. Line up the center grids. You will slide each applique piece, right side up, under the overlay but on top of the background, one piece at a time. It is easy to tell when the applique pieces are in position under the overlay.

1950's Santa Claus

Block #6

Block #2

Block #3

Block #12

Pin your applique pieces in place using 1/2" sequin pins. We generally position and stitch only one or two pieces at a time. Remove the vinyl overlay before stitching.

When you are ready to put away the overlay, lay the tissue paper over the drawn side before you fold it. The tissue paper keeps the lines from transfering from one part of the vinyl to another. Refer to The Applique Handbook by Piece O' Cake for illustrations of this technique.

Positioning Overlay with Fusible Applique

Make the overlay as directed above. Lay your background right side up on your ironing board. Use the overlay to position the applique pieces you want to fuse – often you can position many pieces at once. Carefully remove the overlay. Iron the applique pieces in place. Do not touch the overlay vinyl with the iron because it will melt.

Templates for Hand Applique

Each applique shape requires a template. We have a different way to make templates that is both easy and accurate. Make 2-5 copies of each block on a copier. Compare your copies with the original to insure that they are accurate. From these copies cut out each shape that you need a template for. Leave a little paper allowance around these shapes. Where one shape lays over another cut the top shape from one sheet and the bottom shape from another sheet.

Take one clear self-laminating sheet and lay it shiny side down on the table in front of you. Peel the paper backing off leaving the sticky side up. Carefully stick each template with the drawn side down to the laminate. Use more laminating sheets as necessary.

Cut out each template. Try to split the drawn line – don't cut inside or outside of the line. Keep edges smooth and points sharp.

You'll notice how easy these templates are to cut out. That's the main reason we like this method. It is also true that a mechanical copy of the pattern is more accurate than hand tracing onto template plastic. As you use the templates you will see that they are sturdy and hold up to multiple uses.

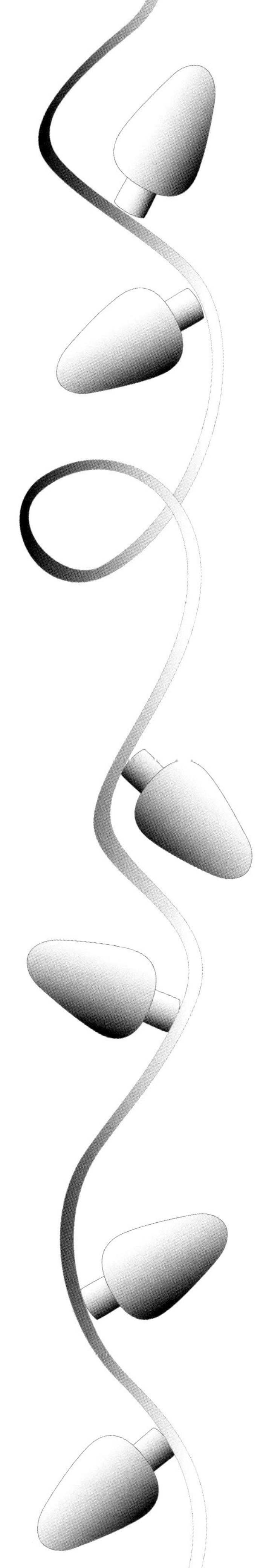

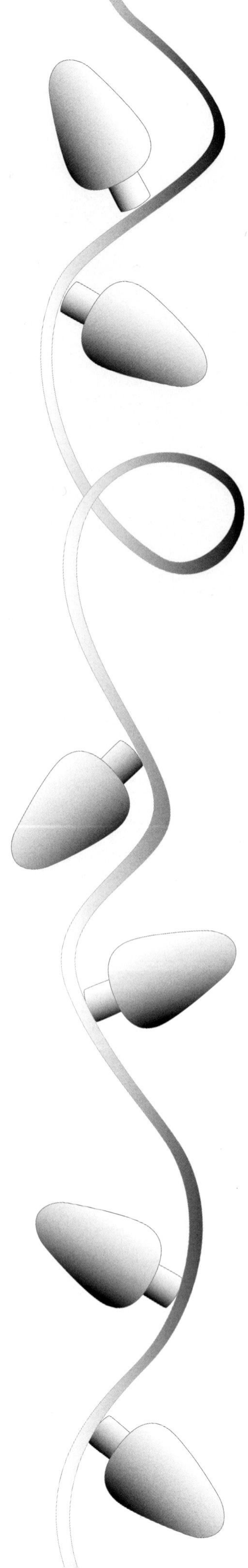

Using Templates in Hand Applique

Templates are used right side up, on the right side of the fabric in needleturn hand applique. Lay your applique fabric right side up on a sandpaper board. Lay your template right side up on the fabric. Lay the template so that as many edges as possible are on the diagonal grain of the fabric. (A bias edge is easier to turn under than one that is on the straight of grain.) Trace around the template. Cut each piece out, adding a 3/16" seam allowance.

Finger press the seam allowance of the applique pieces under before positioning them on your block. This is a very important step. As you finger press, make sure that the drawn line is finger pressed to the back. You'll be amazed at how much easier this one step makes needleturning the seam allowance.

Hand applique your pieces in place with an invisible stitch and matching thread. Refer to <u>The Applique Handbook</u> by Piece O' Cake for more details on needleturn applique.

Templates for Fusible Applique

When you are going to fuse your applique make your templates as stated above with one exception. Stick the <u>blank</u> side of the paper copies to the sticky side of the laminate.

Using Templates in Fusible Applique

Templates are used upside down on the wrong side of the fabric in fusible applique. Following the instructions on your fusible web, iron it to the wrong side of your applique fabric. Do not peel off the paper backing. Lay the fabric right side down. Lay your template upside down and trace around it onto the paper backing. Cut your applique pieces out on the drawn line. Peel off the paper backing. Position the applique pieces on your background fabric and fuse them in place.

After fusing woven cotton fabric we finish the raw edges of the fused applique with a blanket stitch and matching thread on the sewing machine. As the quilts are used, the blanket stitch keeps the edges secure. It is not necessary to blanket stitch the fused felt stockings and tree skirt as they will likely be handled more gently.

Layer, Baste, & Quilt

After your applique is complete, press your blocks on the wrong side. If your ironing surface is hard, lay your blocks on a towel and your applique will not get flattened. Trim your blocks to size. Assemble your quilt top.

Construct the back of the quilt. Lay it right side down. Lay your batting over the back. Smooth any wrinkles. Lay the quilt top right side up over the batting. Baste the layers together.

Quilt your quilt by hand or machine. Finish the outer edge with continuous bias binding (refer to page 71). Sew on any hard embellishments now.

Documentation & Sleeve

Make and attach a sleeve to the back of the quilt.

Make a documentation patch and sew it to the back of the quilt. Include information that you want people to know about your quilt. Your name and address, the date, the fiber content of the quilt, if it was made for a special person or occasion – these are all things that can go on the documentation patch.

Special Techniques

Several helpful techniques are illustrated on pages 67-72 in this book.

Try using the cutaway applique technique on small or unusually shaped applique pieces. If you have never needleturn appliqued a circle, try our method. Practice reverse applique on the train windows.

The vine-like cord for the Christmas tree lights on the borders of The Christmas Trees is easy if you make a continuous bias stem. First you make a length of continuous bias (page 71). Next you make the continuous bias stem (page 72.)

Continuous bias binding is a lovely edge for any quilt. It's worth the effort to learn this easy technique so that your bindings match your quilt. We show you how to master those tricky binding corners on page 71.

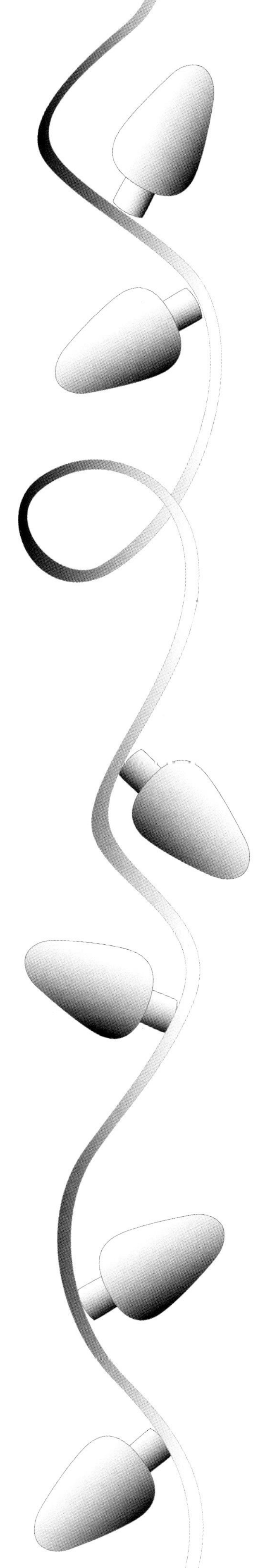

1950's Santa Claus

Yardage & Cutting

FINISHED SIZE – 53" x 66"

BACKGROUND FABRICS

Linda used a variety of background fabrics.

You need an approximate total of 1 5/8 yards for backgrounds.

You need an approximate total of 3/8 yard for the grounds/floors.

Cut as follows:

BLOCKS #1 AND #5 – 14" squares

BLOCKS #2 AND #11 – 12 1/4" x 14" background
2 1/4" x 14" ground/floor

BLOCKS #3, #8, AND #10 – 11 3/4" x 14" background
2 3/4" x 14" ground/floor

BLOCK #4 – 8" x 14" background
6 1/2" x 14" floor

BLOCK #6 – 10 1/4" x 14" background
4 1/4" x 14" floor

BLOCK #7 – 11" x 14" background
3 1/2" x 14" ground/floor

BLOCK #9 – 11 1/2" x 14" background
3" x 14" ground

BLOCK #12 – 12 1/2" x 14" background
2" x 14" ground

Sew grounds/floors to background on the sewing machine.

Trim all blocks to 12 1/2" square when applique is complete.

SASHING FABRIC – 1/2 yard

Cut eight 1 1/2" x 12 1/2" strips

Cut five 1 1/2" x 38 1/2" strips

Cut three 1 1/2" x 40" strips

From this long strip, cut two 1 1/2" x 53 1/2" strips

INNER BORDER FABRIC – 1/8 yard

Cut two 1" x 40 1/2" strips

Cut three 1" x 40" strips. Sew them together end to end.

From this long strip, cut two 1" x 54 1/2" strips.

OUTER BORDER FABRIC – 1 5/8 yards

Cut the following strips from the length of the fabric.

Cut two 8" x 43" strips for top and bottom borders.

Trim to 6 1/2" x 41 1/2" after applique is complete.

Cut two 8" x 56" strips for side borders.

Trim to 6 1/2" x 54 1/2" after applique is complete.

6 1/2" OHIO STAR BLOCKS – 1/8 yard of each of the following

See page 14 for piecing instructions.

Cut four 3 1/2" squares for the star centers

Cut thirty-two 2" squares for the star points

Cut sixteen 2" squares for the corners of the blocks

Cut sixteen 2" x 3 1/2" rectangles for the sides of the blocks

BINDING FABRIC – 3/4 yard (see page 71)

Make 2 1/2" wide continuous bias binding.

BACKING AND SLEEVE FABRIC – 4 yards

Make Santa's Quilt

Piece Santa's quilt in block number 4 like Linda did. It really makes this block special!

1. Cut ten 1 1/2" x 12" strips from different fabrics. Sew them together. Press all seam allowances in the same direction.

2. Cut eight 1 1/2" strips.

3. Turn every other strip upside down. Shift strips as shown above. Sew them together. Cut the quilt from the center of this unit.

Assemble the Quilt

1. Read the instructions at the front of this book.
2. Sew the grounds/floors and backgrounds together.
3. Applique the Santa blocks and the borders.
4. Do the embroidery.
5. Press the blocks on the wrong side and trim them to size.
6. Make the Ohio Star blocks.
7. Set the quilt together (see diagram below).
   Sash the blocks and short sashing together into rows.
   Sew rows together with the five 38 1/2" sashing strips.
   Sew on the two side sashing strips.
   Sew on the top and bottom inner border strips.
   Sew on the side inner border strips.
   Sew on the top and bottom outer borders.
   Sew an Ohio Star to each end of the side outer borders.
   Sew the side outer borders onto the quilt.
8. Follow the instructions in the front of this book to finish the quilt.
9. Add hard embellishements and ribbon after the quilting is complete.

Piece the Ohio Stars

1. Draw a diagonal line on the wrong side of the 2" square star points.

2. Lay a 2" square over one half of a 2" x 31/2" rectangle, right sides together. Sew on the drawn line.

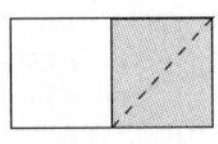

3. Cut off the excess fabric 1/4" away from your seam line, as shown below. Press open.

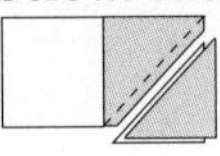

4. Lay a 2" square over the other half of the rectangle, right sides together. Sew on the drawn line.

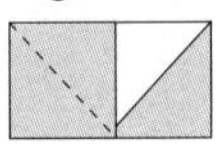

5. Cut off the excess fabric 1/4" away from your seam line, as shown below. Press open.

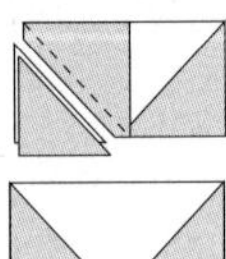

6. Lay out your pieced units and corner squares. Sew them together into three rows as shown below. Sew rows together to finish the star. This block is 6 1/2". Make three more Ohio Stars.

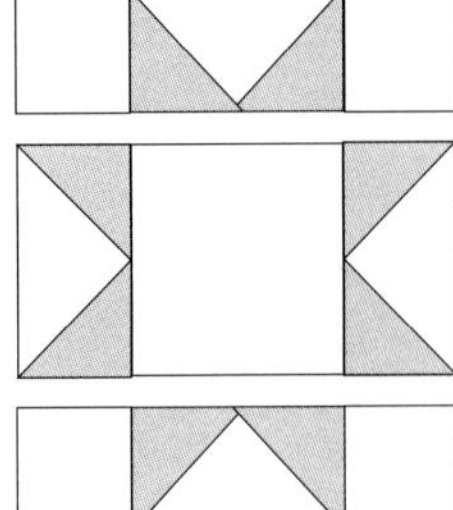

The Santa Blocks

The patterns for the Santa blocks are too big to fit on one page. Make copies of the drawings of the blocks on pages 15-33. Compare your copies with the original to insure that they are accurate. Tape together the two sides of each block.

The blocks in the quilt are numbered from left to right, top to bottom. For example, Block #1 is located in the upper left hand corner of the quilt.

The small dashed lines on the patterns indicate the vertical and horizontal centers. The larger dashed lines indicate the place where the two sides of the pattern meet.

A few applique pieces (like Santa's beard) will sometimes be divided into two parts, with a different number on each part. In that case, stitch down the side of the piece with the lowest number. Stitch down the next applique piece(s) in numerical sequence. Stitch down the second half of the applique piece when it's number comes up.

Special Instructions for the Faces

Lay muslin over the drawing of each face. Use permanent gel or paint pens and trace the eyes. Look at the book cover to see how Linda used her pens. Use a pink pen and color in the area where Santa's mouth is. The beard and mustache will cover the edges of the mouth.

Special Instructions for the Santa Border

MAKE THE PATTERN FOR THE BORDERS. Cut two pieces of paper 6" X 41" for the top and bottom borders. With a ruler, draw the center horizontal and vertical lines. Trace the patterns for the train on pages 35-38 onto these pieces of paper. Refer to the photograph of the quilt on page 7. Make sure that you keep the train at least 1/4" away from the outer edges of the paper, as these are the finished edges of the border.

Cut two pieces of paper 6" x 54" for the side borders. Draw the center lines as above. Trace the patterns for the toys onto your paper. Again, make sure that you don't get too close to the outer edges.

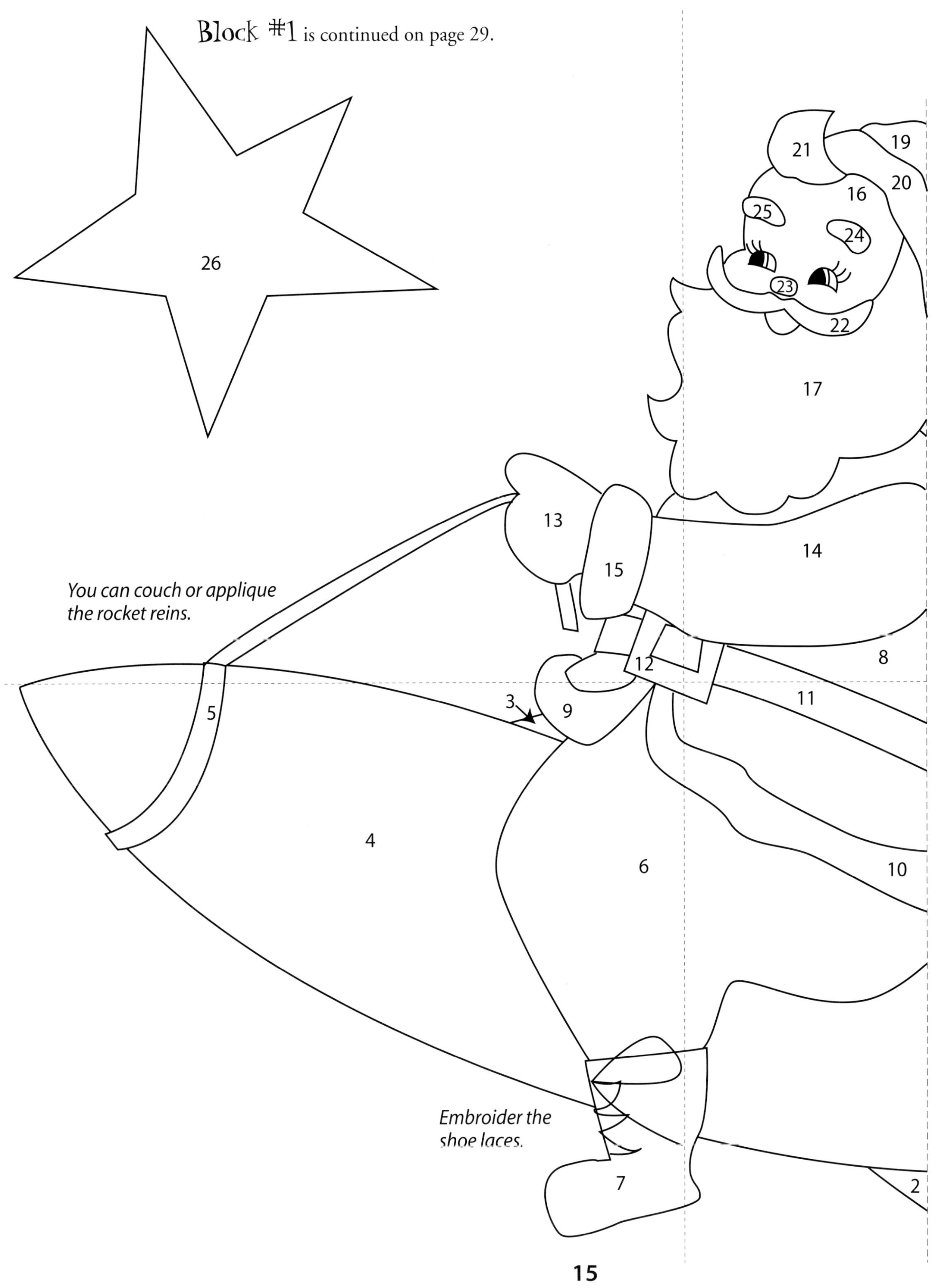

Block #1 is continued on page 29.
26
21
19
20
16
25
24
23
22
17
14
13
15
12
8
You can couch or applique
the rocket reins.
5
3
9
11
4
6
10
Embroider the
shoe laces.
7
2

Block #2 is continued on page 30.

Santa's beard is divided into two parts.
First stitch down the part of the beard
with the lowest number. Continue
stitching in numerical order.

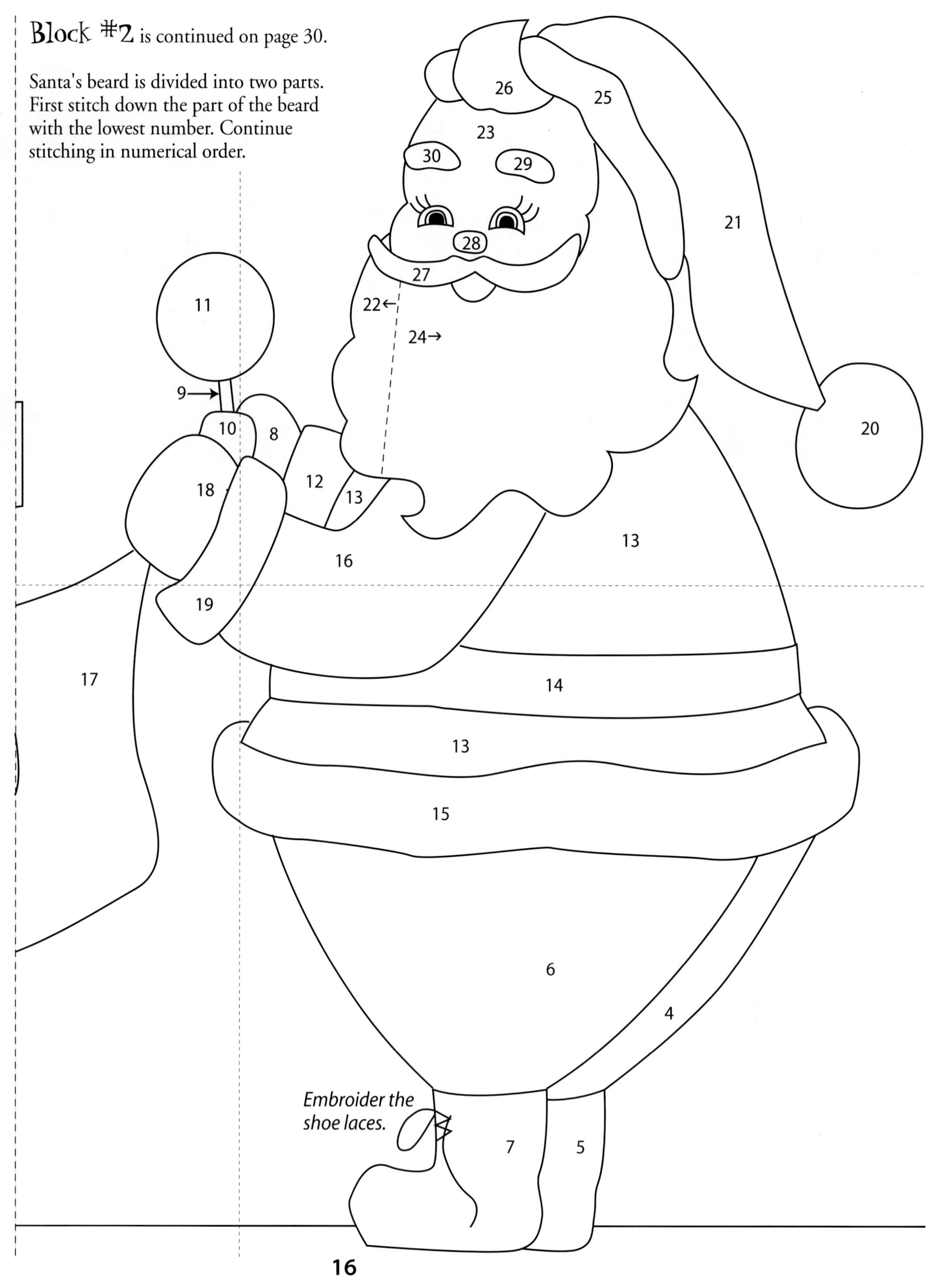

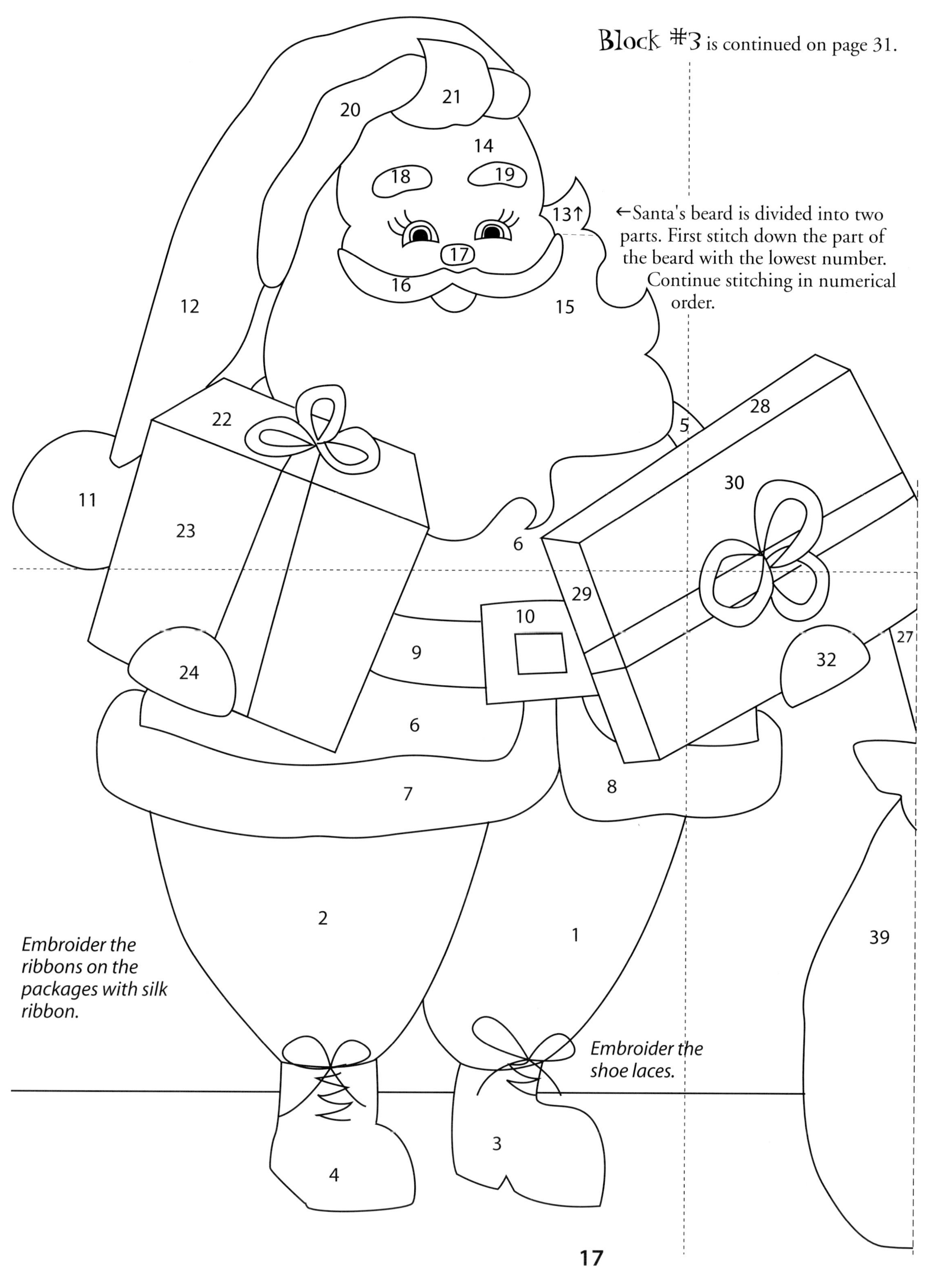

Block #3 is continued on page 31.
←Santa's beard is divided into two parts. First stitch down the part of the beard with the lowest number. Continue stitching in numerical order.
Embroider the ribbons on the packages with silk ribbon.
Embroider the shoe laces.
20
21
14
18
19
13↑
12
17
16
15
22
5
28
11
23
30
6
29
10
24
9
27
6
32
7
8
2
1
39
4
3

Block #4 is continued on page 32.

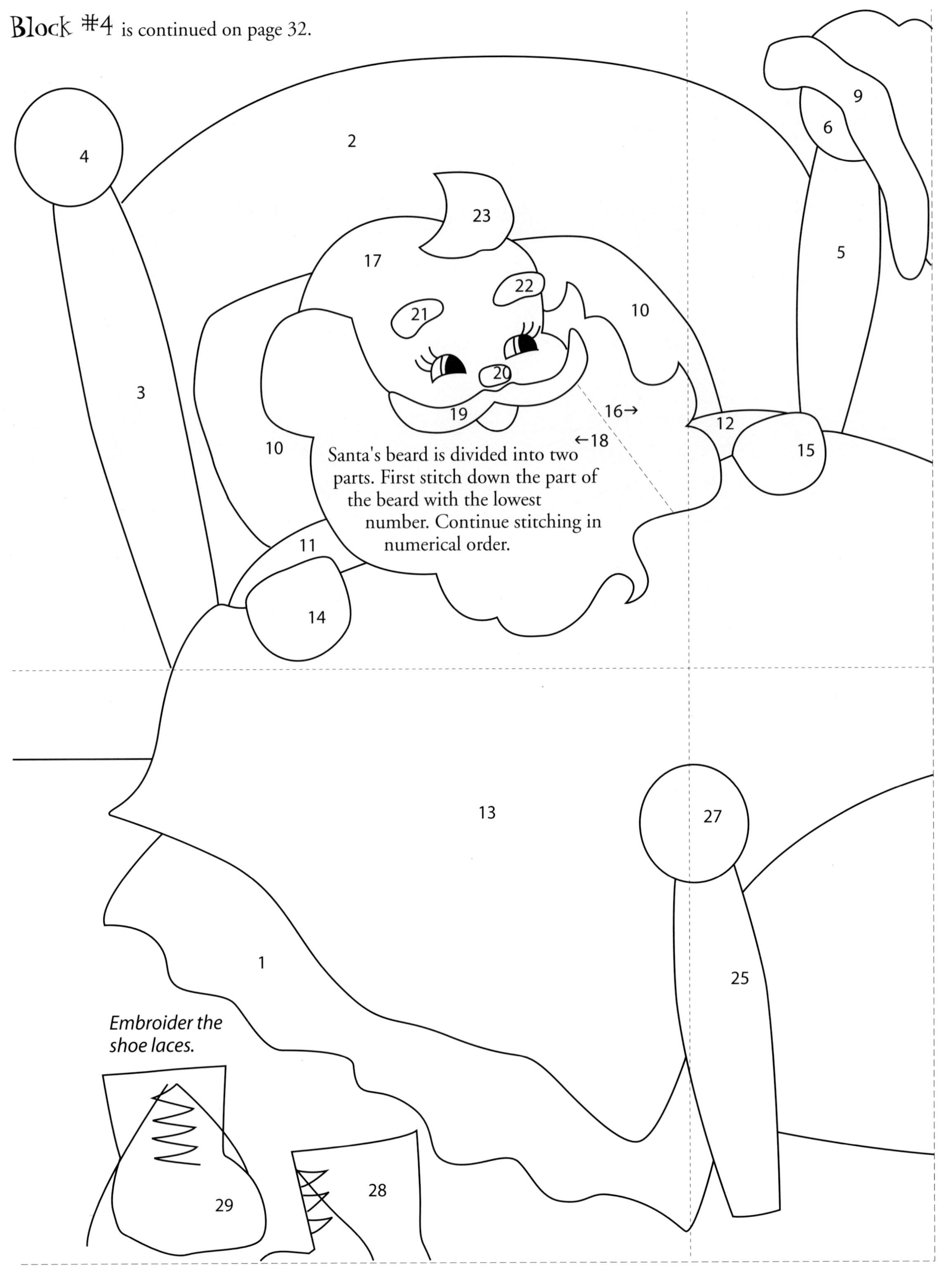

Block #5 is continued on page 33.

Dear Santa,
I have bin good t
year. Mom sez so 2.
t think you should br
alot of toys.

And a puppy! I
my cat Socks wi
nice to her.

Linda backstitched her letter.
Put a special name on your letter block using the alphabet on page 38.

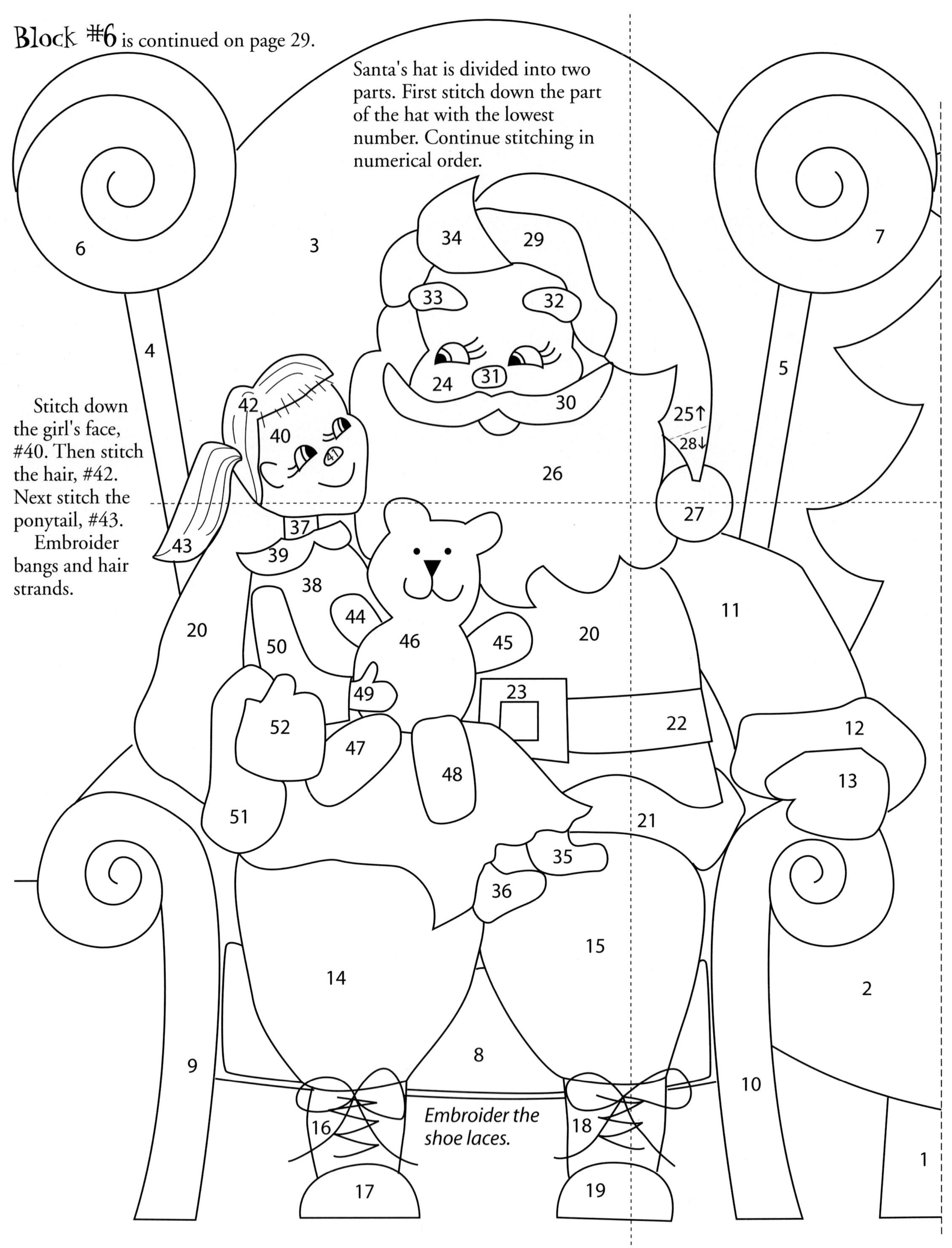

Block #6 is continued on page 29.
Santa's hat is divided into two parts. First stitch down the part of the hat with the lowest number. Continue stitching in numerical order.
Stitch down the girl's face, #40. Then stitch the hair, #42. Next stitch the ponytail, #43. Embroider bangs and hair strands.
Embroider the shoe laces.

Block #7 is continued on page 33.

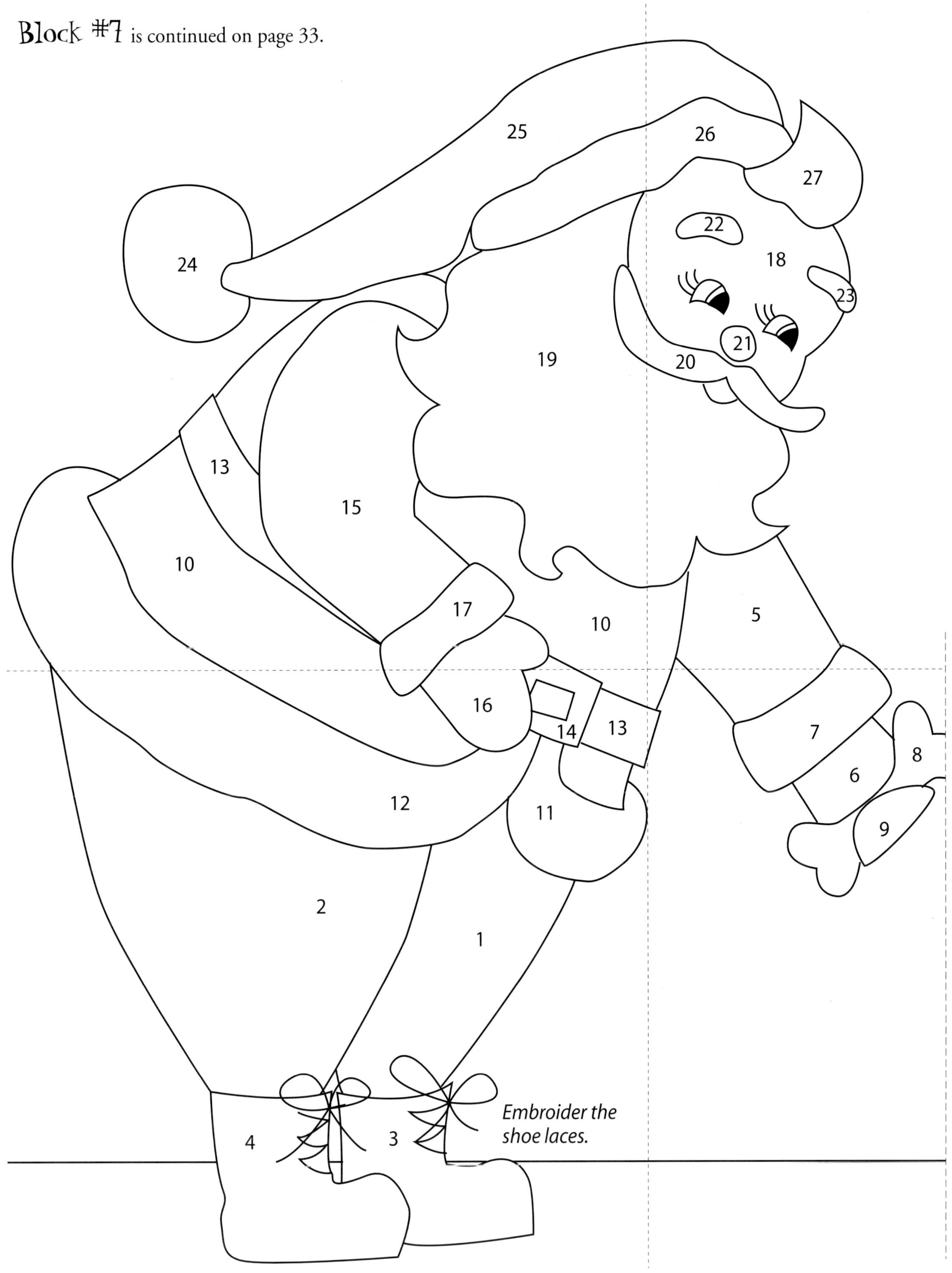

Block #8 is continued on page 30.

Santa's beard is divided into two parts. First stitch down the part of the beard with the lowest number. Continue stitching in numerical order.

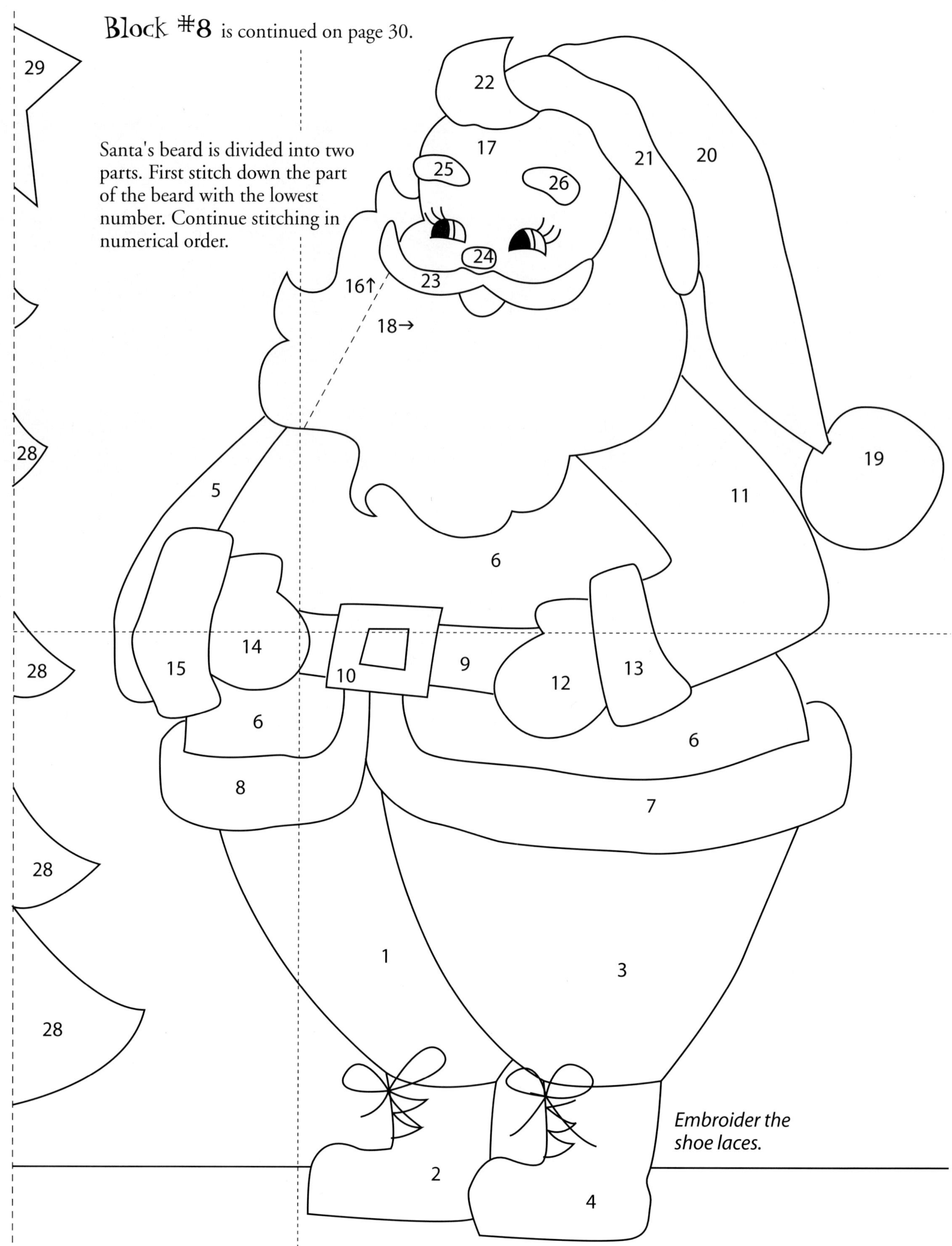

Block #9 is continued on page 32.
Santa's beard and the candy cane are each divided into two parts. First stitch down the part of the beard with the lowest number. Continue stitching in numerical order. Repeat for candy cane.
Embroider the snow woman's arm.
Embroider the shoe laces.
21
25
17
24
20
15
16↑
18→
23
22
14
5
19↑
10↓
12
31
9
8
11
13
32
6
7
30
33
1
3
2
4
26
27
28
29
26

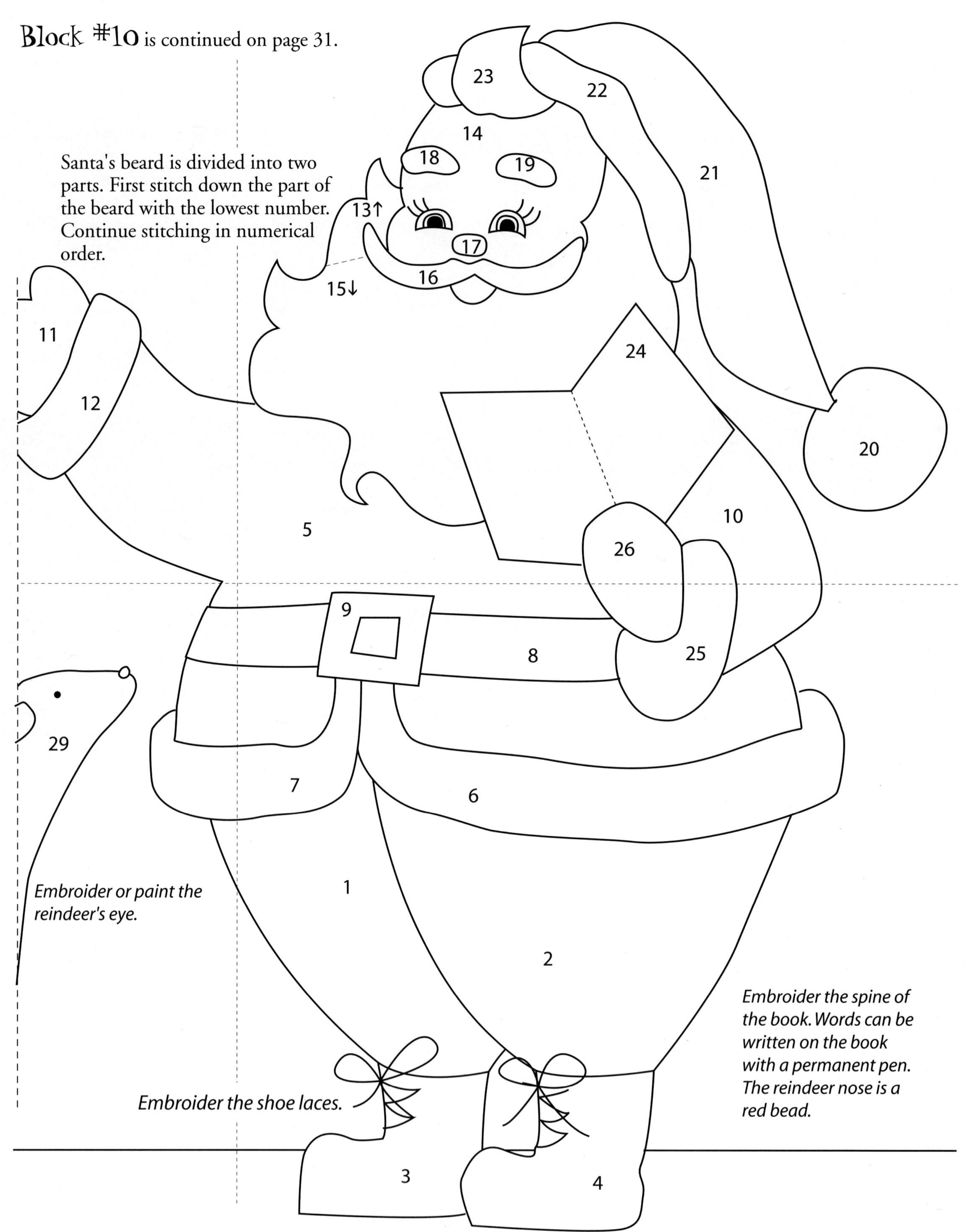

Block #10 is continued on page 31.
Santa's beard is divided into two parts. First stitch down the part of the beard with the lowest number. Continue stitching in numerical order.
Embroider or paint the reindeer's eye.
Embroider the shoe laces.
Embroider the spine of the book. Words can be written on the book with a permanent pen. The reindeer nose is a red bead.

The Christmas Trees Table Runner

1950's Stockings and Rocket Tree Skirt

Embroidery Fun!

Embroidered projects are fast, easy, & fun! The projects on this page utilize the alphabet (page 38) from the 1950's Santa Claus quilt.

Block #11 is continued on page 34.

Santa's beard is divided into two parts. First stitch down the part of the beard with the lowest number. Continue stitching in numerical order.

Embroider the shoe laces.

Block #12 is continued on page 34.
*Piece #28 is tricky. Position it in sequence, but only sew down the edge that falls over the hat. The arm is sewn over the right end of #28 with the seam allowance on the face edge folded under. Next position and sew the beard and then finish the hat trim.
Right edge of block. →
Open the seam between the ground and sky. Insert the base of the tree trunk. Sew the snow over it.

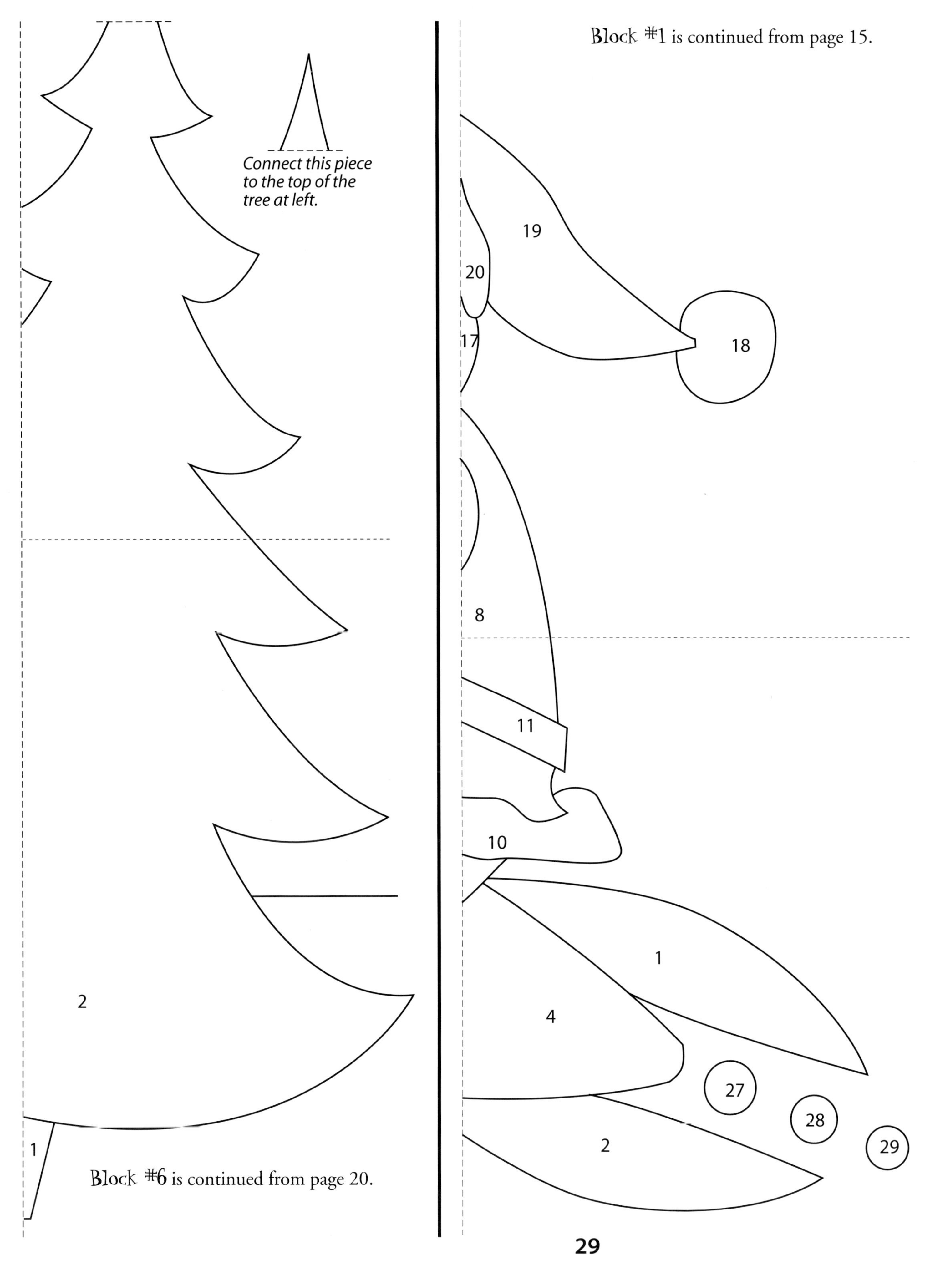

Block #1 is continued from page 15.

Block #6 is continued from page 20.

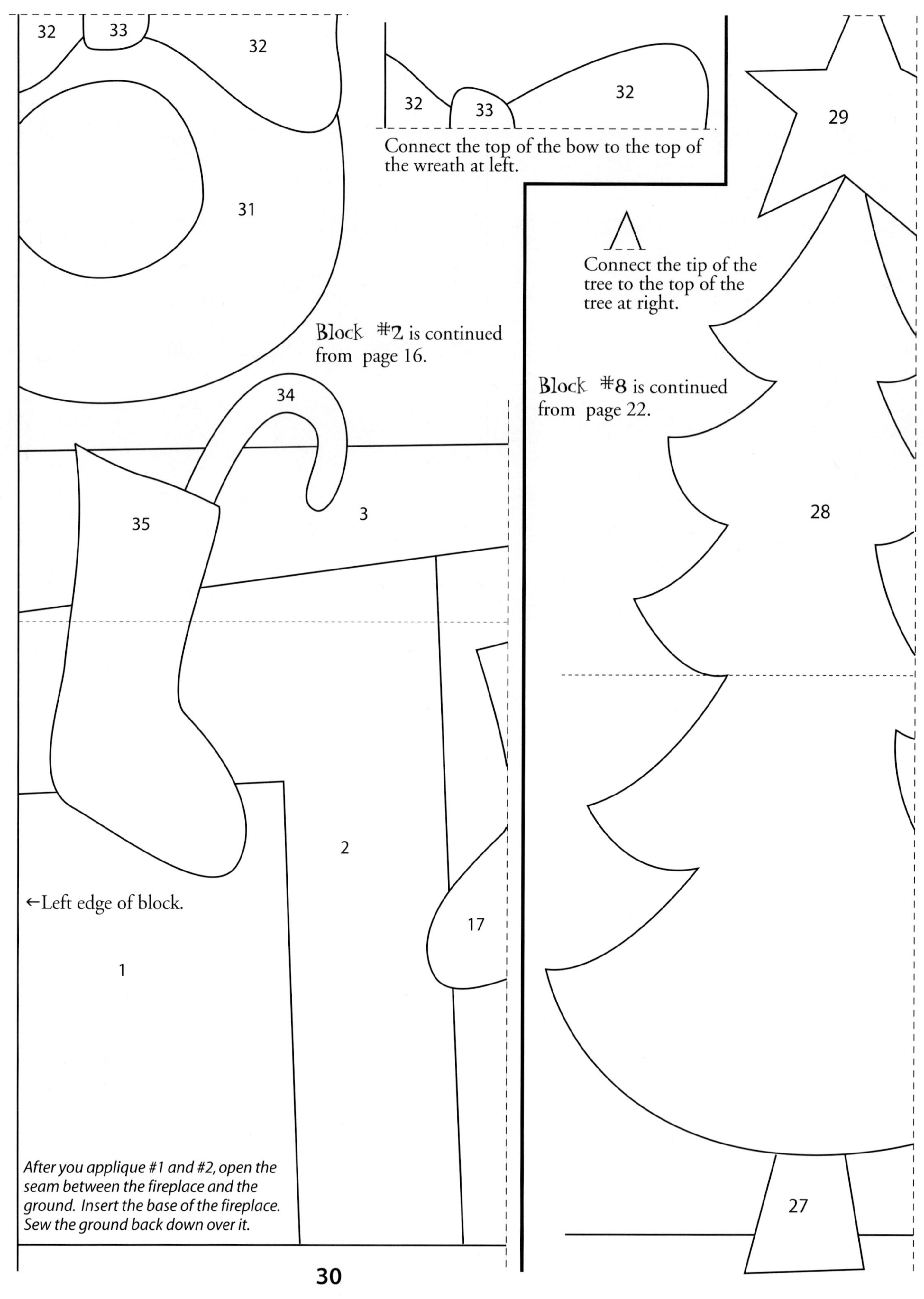

32
33
32
31
32
33
32
Connect the top of the bow to the top of
the wreath at left.
29
Connect the tip of the
tree to the top of the
tree at right.
Block #2 is continued
from page 16.
Block #8 is continued
from page 22.
34
35
3
28
2
17
←Left edge of block.
1
After you applique #1 and #2, open the
seam between the fireplace and the
ground. Insert the base of the fireplace.
Sew the ground back down over it.
27

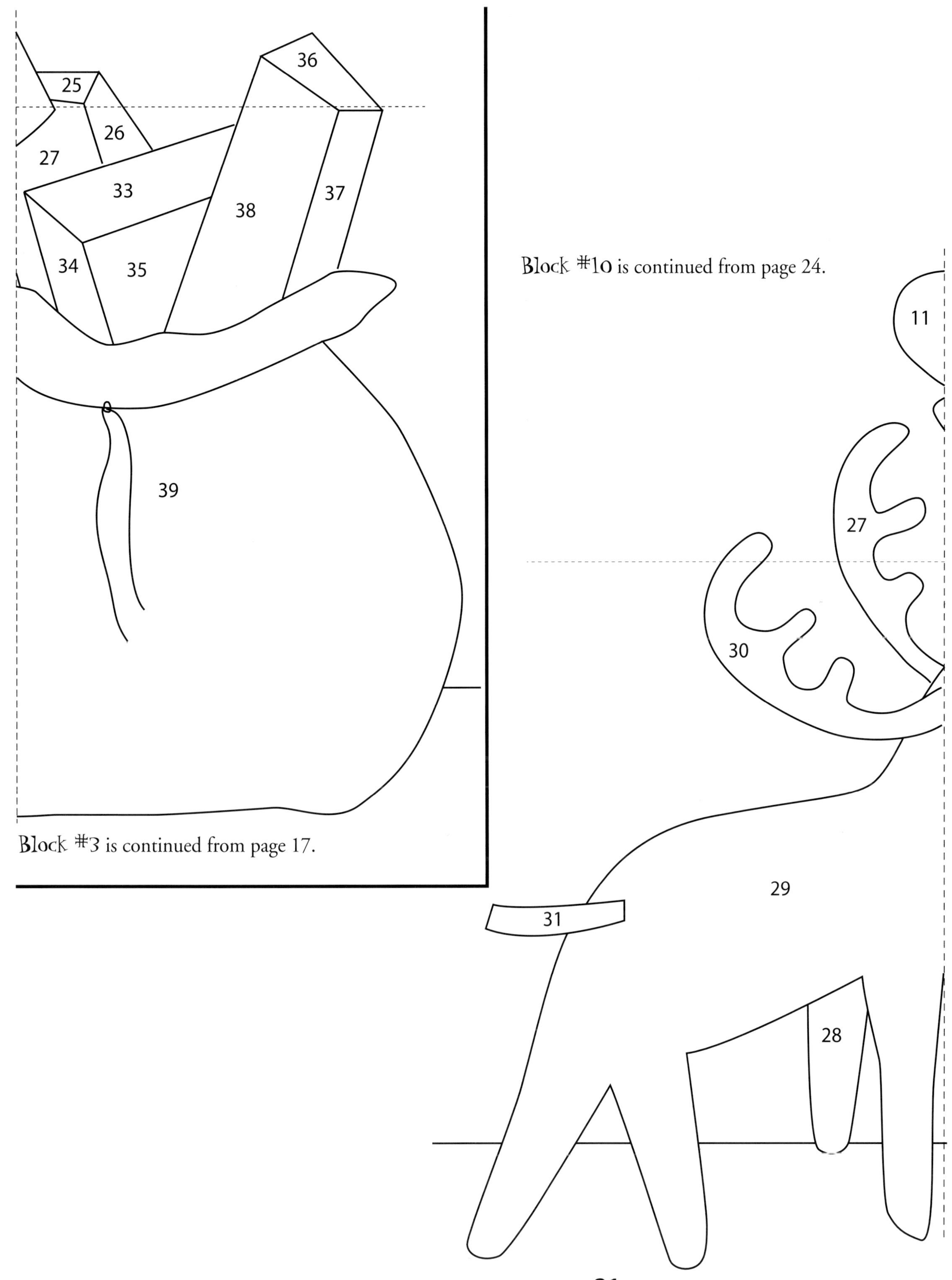

Block #10 is continued from page 24.

Block #3 is continued from page 17.

Block #4 is continued from page 18.

28

Add to shoe at bottom
of Block #4.

34

34

35

27

Connect this piece
to the top of the
flower above, right.

28

Block #9 is continued from page 32

8

26

7

26

31

30

28

24

26

26

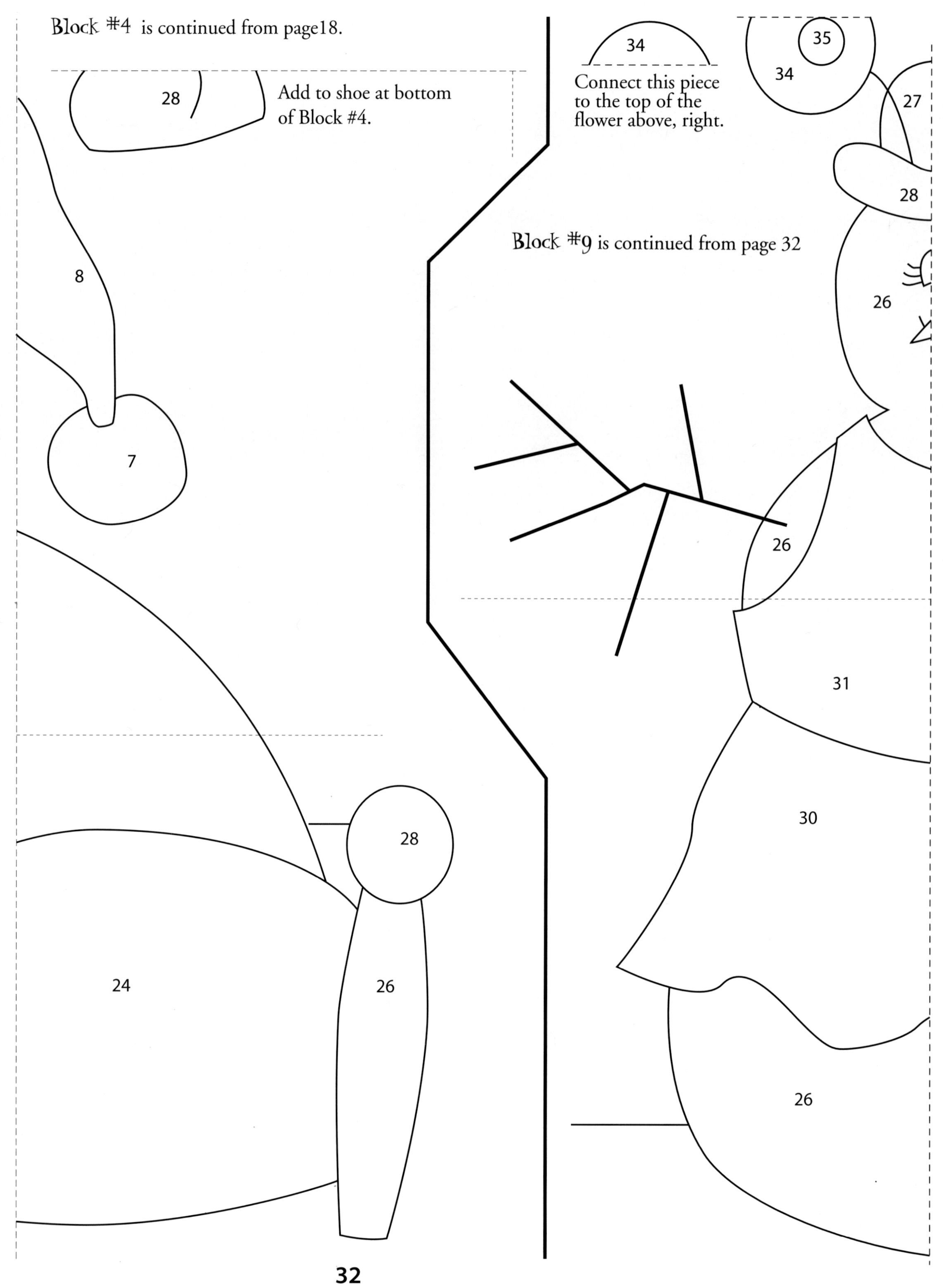

Block #7 is continued from page 21.

Block #5 continued from page 19.

8

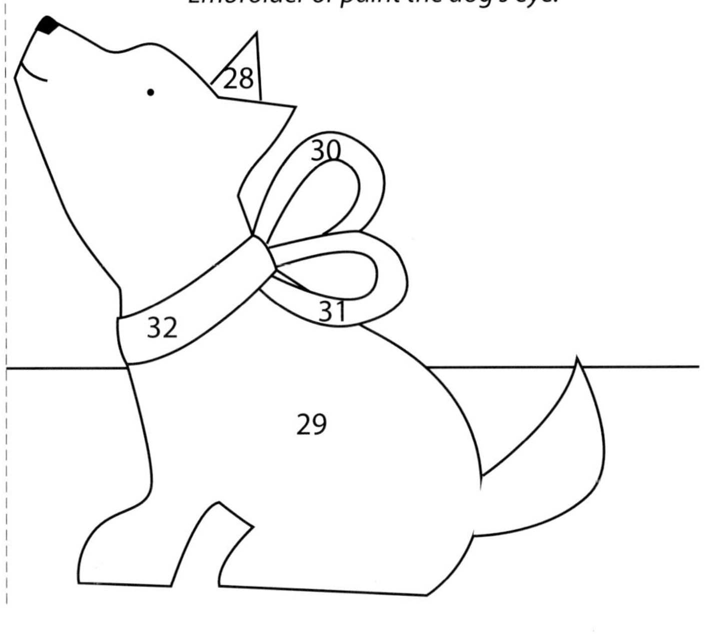

Embroider or paint the dog's eye.

his

So I

ing me

promise

ll be

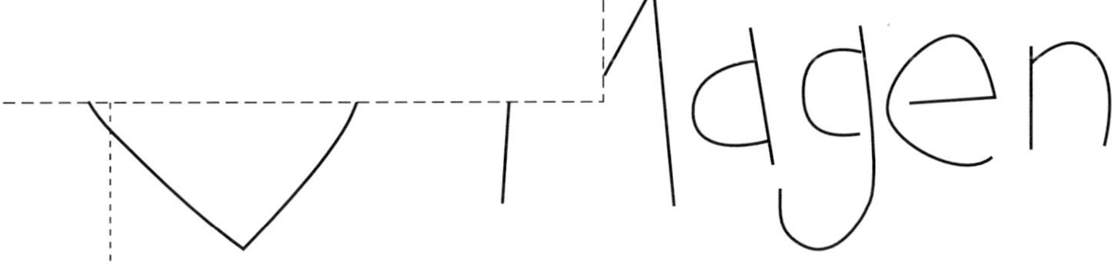

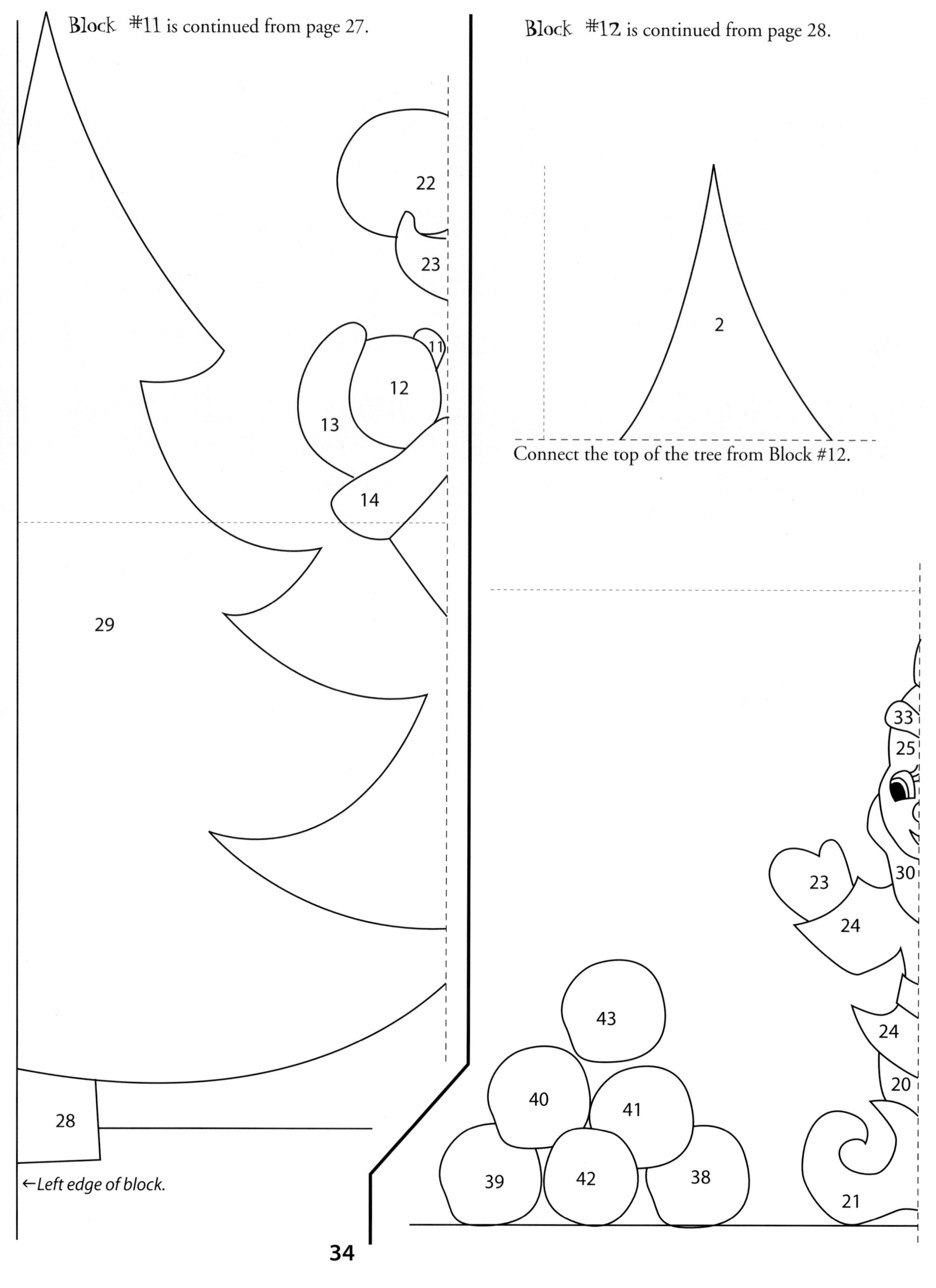

Block #11 is continued from page 27.
Block #12 is continued from page 28.
22
23
11
12
13
14
2
Connect the top of the tree from Block #12.
29
33
25
23
30
24
43
40
41
24
20
28
39
42
38
21
←Left edge of block.
34

Toys and Train Cars for the Outer Border
The train on the top border is reversed. To get the reverse image, turn your templates upside down and then trace around them on the right side of your fabric.
Train Engine
Embroider the lines in the windows.
Train Caboose
Train Package Car #2
Use silk ribbon for the package bow.
Embroider the bear's face.
Bear w/Bow Tie

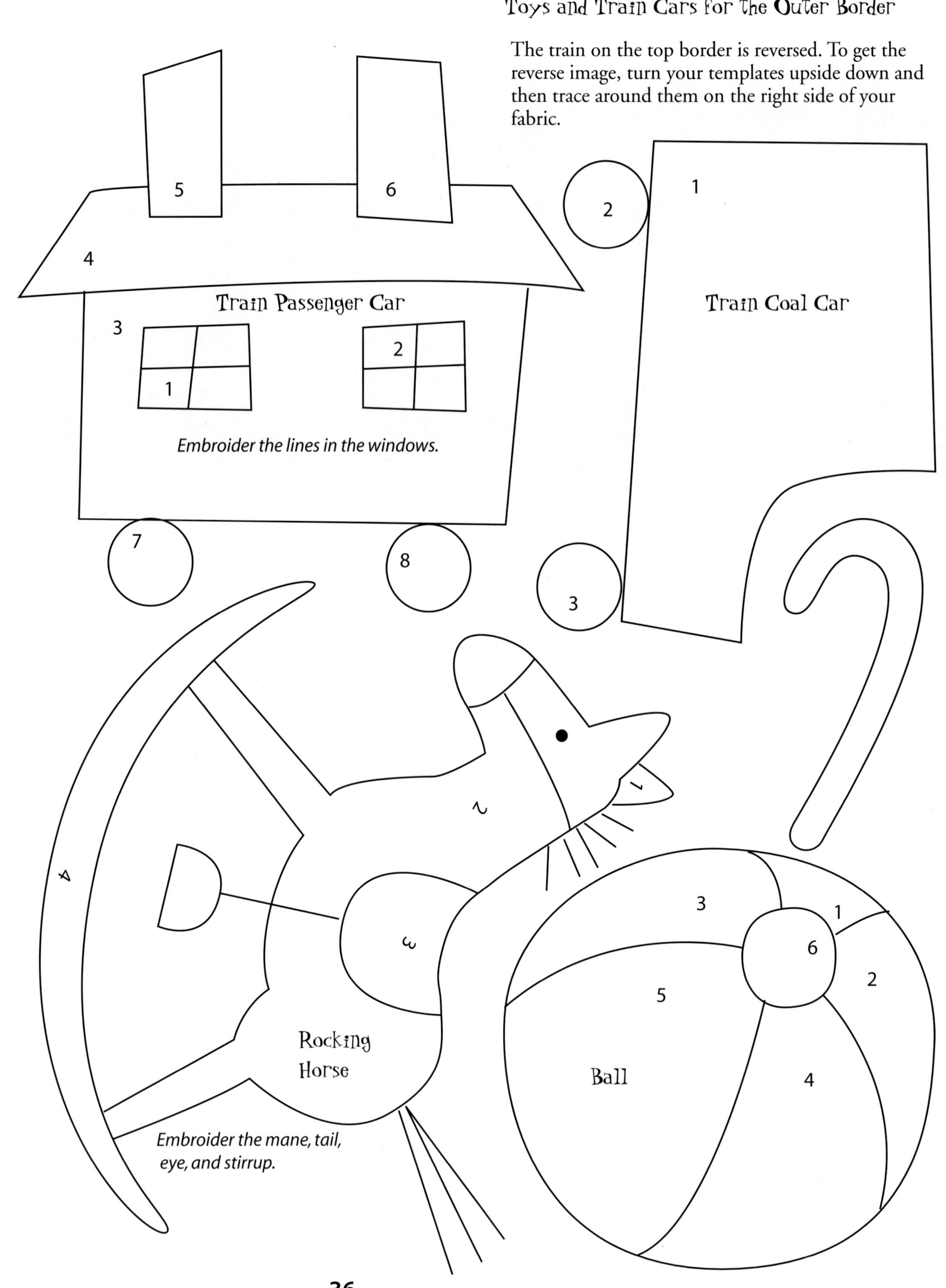

Toys and Train Cars for the Outer Border
The train on the top border is reversed. To get the reverse image, turn your templates upside down and then trace around them on the right side of your fabric.
5
6
4
Train Passenger Car
3
2
1
Embroider the lines in the windows.
7
8
2
1
3
Train Coal Car
1
Rocking
Horse
Embroider the mane, tail, eye, and stirrup.
Ball
3
1
6
2
5
4

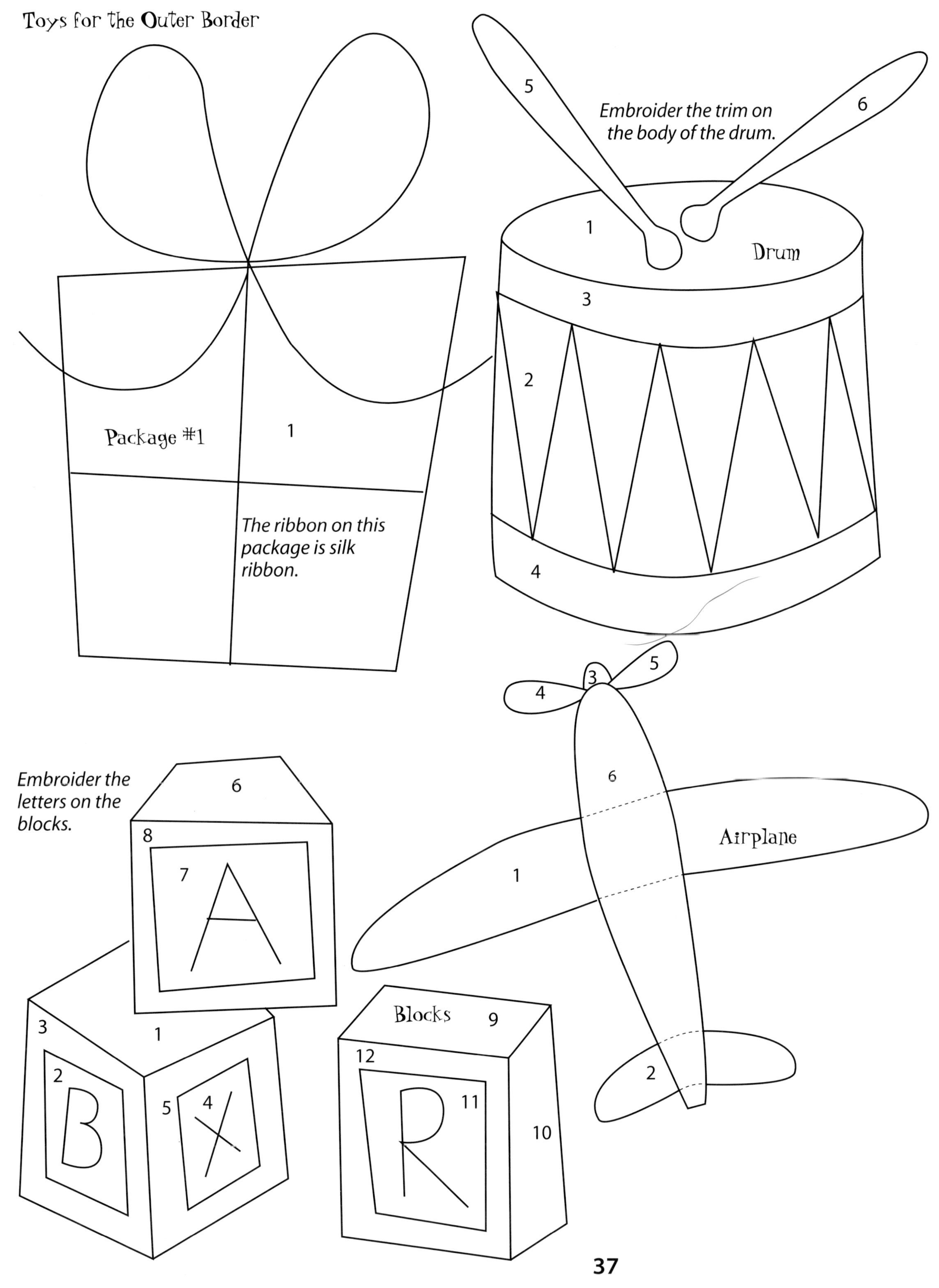
Package #1
1
The ribbon on this package is silk ribbon.
Embroider the trim on the body of the drum.
5
6
1
Drum
3
2
4
3
4
5
Embroider the letters on the blocks.
6
8
7
A
3
1
2
B
5
4
X
Blocks
9
12
R
11
10
Airplane
6
1
2

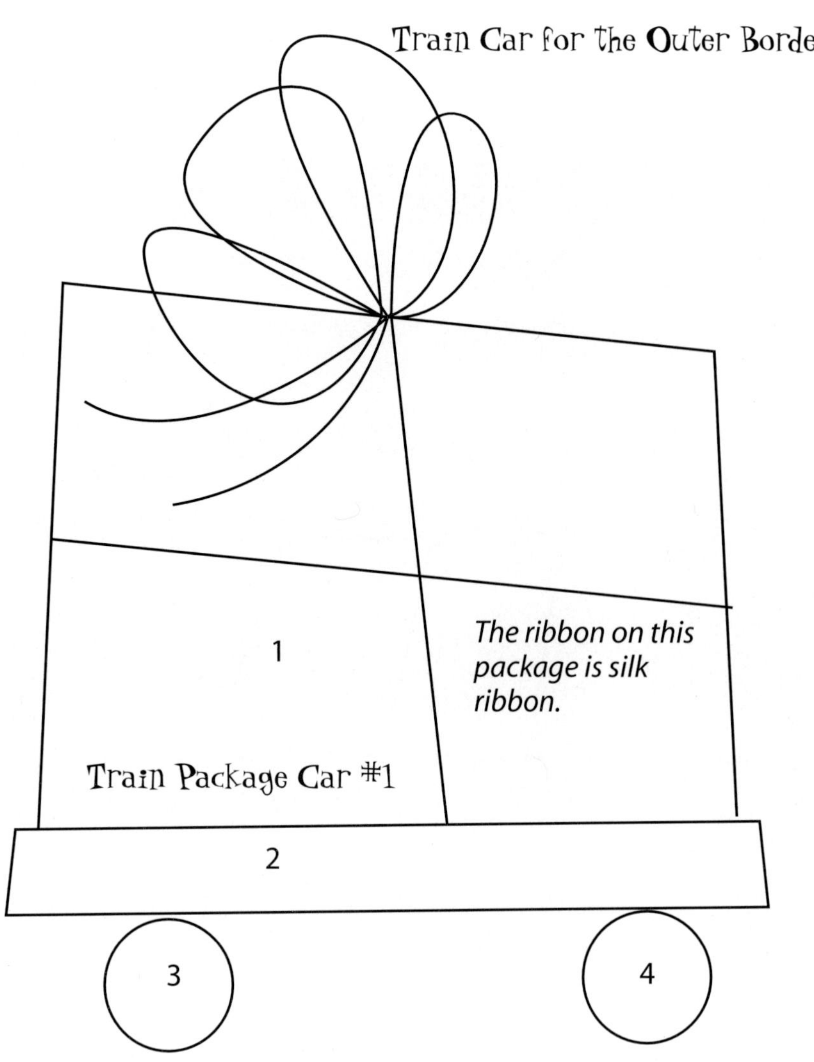

Framed Letter to Santa

Embroider a letter to Santa to frame for your wall! Ours fits an 11" x 14" frame (see photo on page 26).

1. Cut a 17" x 20" piece of background fabric.
2. Transfer your special letter to Santa using the alphabet below.
3. Embroider your letter with a backstitch. Press it from the wrong side over a plush towel.
4. Stretch the letter over a padded foam core board.
5. Frame it and hang it on your wall.

a b c d e f g h i j k l m n o p q r s
t u v w x y z A B C D E F
G H I J K L M N O P
Q R S T U V W X Y Z

Christmas Stockings

Christmas stockings make great gifts for family and friends both. Becky's Aunt Helen made an authentic Fifties stocking for Becky when she was a baby decorated with sequins and beads. Becky uses it every year. See our version on page 25.

STOCKING BACK – one fat quarter of felt

STOCKING FRONT – 1/2 yard of felt

FELT APPLIQUES – small pieces of felt in a variety of colors

NOTIONS –
Sequins, beads, etc.
Fusible web

Attach fusible web to the back of the felt before cutting out the pieces.

Use elements from any block in this book to design your stockings. Fuse, glue, and/or sew appliques and embellishments in place.

Put name here.

Fifties Felt Stockings:

1. Trace this pattern and enlarge it by 200% on a copier. A 1/4" seam allowance is included.

2. Use the enlarged pattern to cut a front and back out of felt for each stocking.
Pink the edges of the front fabric.

3. Decorate the front of the stocking before sewing the stocking together.

4. Either sew the name directly to the stocking front or cut a rectangle of felt in a contrasting color for the name plate (see above). Pink the edges. Make the name with sequins, embroidery floss, glue and glitter – use your imagination! Fuse, glue, or sew the name plate in place before sewing the front and back of the stocking together.

5. When your stocking is decorated, fuse a fabric lining to the wrong side of the stocking front. Sew the front to the back, wrong sides together.

6. Make a hanging tab from a 4" length of rick rack or a 1" x 4" piece of felt. Fold the hanging tab in half. Sew the cut ends to the inside of the stocking back, near the "calf" seam.

Have fun decorating the stocking! We used felt for our stockings. Flannel or velvet would be fun to use too. Hunt for interesting, sparkly embellishments like sequins, rick rack, and miniature Christmas tree ornaments to make your stockings special.

Tip: If you are making a "family" of stockings, make sure that all the toes point in the same direction so that they hang nicely together.

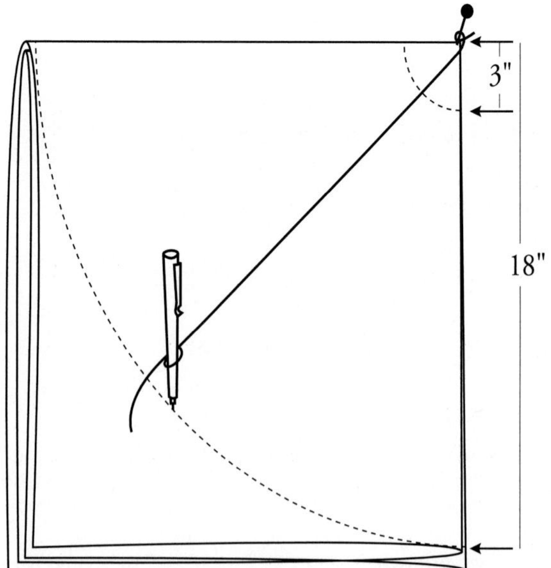

A String Compass

Draw the circles on the felt with a string compass. Begin by folding the felt in half vertically and then horizontally. Insert a pin at the corner away from the raw edges. Attach a string to the pin and to a fine point marker. Hold the pin steady and the pen vertically. Draw the outer circle, then the inner circle. Cut one layer at a time (felt is thick!) using the previous cut as a guide for the next cut.

Rocket Santa Tree Skirt

Make this cute felt tree skirt using the pattern for Block #1. It will send you back to the Fifties! Fuse or glue the applique pieces in place.

BACKGROUND – 1 yard blue felt
Cut one 36" circle
Mark a 6" circle in the center of the larger circle.
SANTA FACES – muslin scraps
Draw three Santa faces on muslin. Attach fusible web to the back of the muslin and cut out the faces.
FELT APPLIQUES – 1/4 yard each of red and yellow felt, 1/8 yard of a variety of other colors
NOTIONS –
4 yards of big rick rack
1 yard of fusible web or fabric glue

If fusing, attach fusible web to the back of the felt before cutting out the pieces. First, test the fusible web on scrap felt to find the right iron temperature. You want to fuse the felt without melting it.

Use the drawing above and your Block #1 placement overlay as a guide. Position the applique pieces on the background. Fuse or glue them in place.

Draw a line on the background connecting the inner circle with the outer edge. Cut along this line. Cut out the inner circle. Glue or sew large rick rack to the edges of the inner and outer circles.

A tree skirt is used but once a year, and it doesn't get much wear. Blanket stitch around the applique pieces if you feel it will hold the edges in place better over time.

Use other patterns in the book to make even more Christmas tree skirts!

The Christmas Trees

Yardage & Cutting

Becky used a variety of background fabrics in her quilt. She separated the beige backgrounds into two groups: lighter and darker. She also used several red fabrics. Yardage amounts below are generous.

FINISHED SIZE – 49 1/2" SQUARE

DARKER BEIGE BACKGROUND FABRICS –
You need an approximate total of 1/2 yard.
Cut thirteen 4 1/2" squares (Ohio Star centers)
Cut four strips 1 1/4" x 40 1/2" (inner border)

LIGHTER BEIGE BACKGROUND FABRICS –
You need an approximate total of 3 yards.
Cut fifty-two 2 1/2" squares (Ohio star block corners)
Cut fifty-two 2 1/2" x 4 1/2" rectangles (Ohio star block sides)
Cut twelve 10" squares (tree block backgrounds)
Cut four 6" x 43 1/2" strips (outer border backgrounds)
    Trim to 4 1/2" x 42" after applique is complete.

REDS – 7/8 yard
Cut one hundred fifty-two 2 1/2" squares
    (star points and tree block corners)
Cut four 1 1/4" squares (inner border corners)
Cut four 4 1/2" squares (outer border corners)

CHRISTMAS LIGHT CORD – 3/4 yard brown fabric
Make 3/8" wide continuous bias stem.

A WIDE VARIETY OF FABRIC SCRAPS FOR THE APPLIQUE

CONTINUOUS BIAS BINDING FABRIC – 3/4 yard
    Cut one 23" square to make 2 1/4" wide binding.

BACKING AND SLEEVE FABRIC – 4 yards

SPECIAL TOOLS – Bias stem bars

Piece the Ohio Stars

1. Draw a diagonal line on the wrong side of all of the red 2 1/2" squares. Reserve forty-eight for the tree blocks.

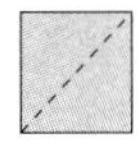

2. Lay a 2 1/2" square over one half of a 2 1/2" x 4 1/2" rectangle star block side, right sides together. Sew on the drawn line. Repeat for all rectangles.

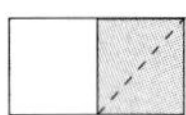

3. Cut off the excess fabric 1/4" away from your seam line, as shown below. Press open.

4. Lay a 2 1/2" square over the other half of the rectangle, right sides together. Sew on the drawn line. Repeat for all rectangles.

5. Cut off the excess fabric 1/4" away from your seam line, as shown below. Press open.

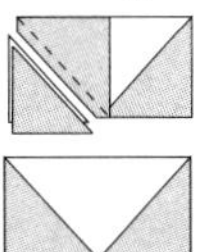

6. Lay out the pieced units, center square, and corner squares. Sew them together into three rows as shown below. Sew rows together to finish the star. This block is 8 1/2" square.

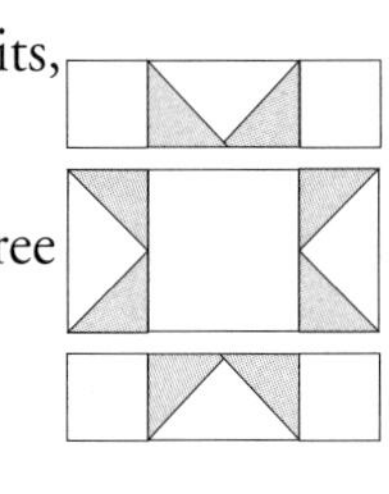

Complete the tree blocks:

After the applique is complete, press the tree blocks from the back and trim them to 8 1/2" square.

Sew a 2 1/2" red square to each corner of each tree block. Trim away excess as shown. Press open.

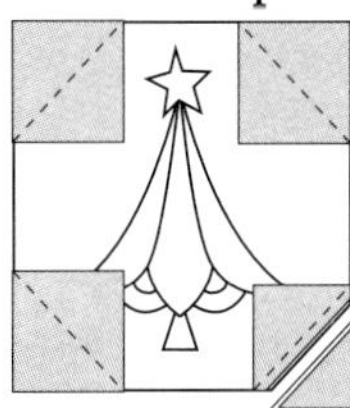

1. Read the instructions at the front of this book.
2. Applique the trees to the 10" squares.
3. Embroider trees that have embroidery embellishments.
4. Press and trim the tree blocks to 8 1/2". Complete the tree blocks
5. Make the Ohio Star blocks.
6. Applique the outer borders.
7. Press and trim the borders to 4 1/2" x 42".
8. Set the quilt together (see diagram below).
   Sew the blocks together into rows.
   Sew rows together.
   Sew on the two side inner borders.
   Sew a small red square to either end of the top and bottom inner border strips. Sew them to the quilt.
   Sew on the side outer border strips.
   Sew a large red square to either end of the top and bottom borders. Sew them to the quilt.
9. Follow the instructions in the front of this book (page 11) to finish the quilt.

The Tree Blocks

The blocks are numbered from left to right, top to bottom. For example, Block #1 is located in the upper left hand corner of the quilt.

The block patterns are placed on the following pages so as to conserve space. The horizontal and vertical centers are marked on each with a dashed line. Use these patterns as directed in the general instructions at the front of this book.

Block #5
8
7
6
5
4
3
2
1
3
7
7
7
7
2
7
7
1
Block #2
6
5
4
Embroider a
swag on the
dashed line.

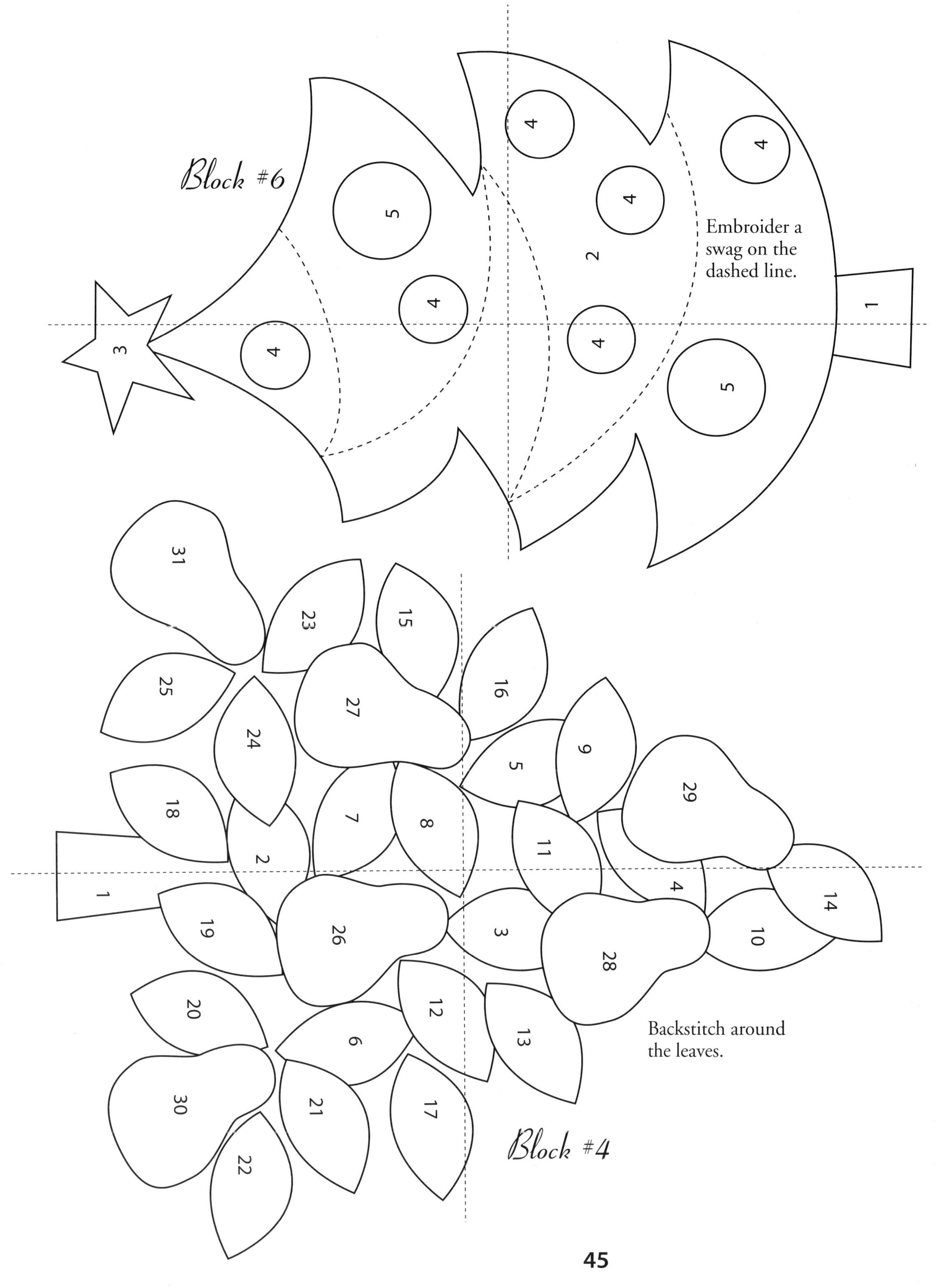

Block #6
Embroider a swag on the dashed line.
Backstitch around the leaves.
Block #4

45

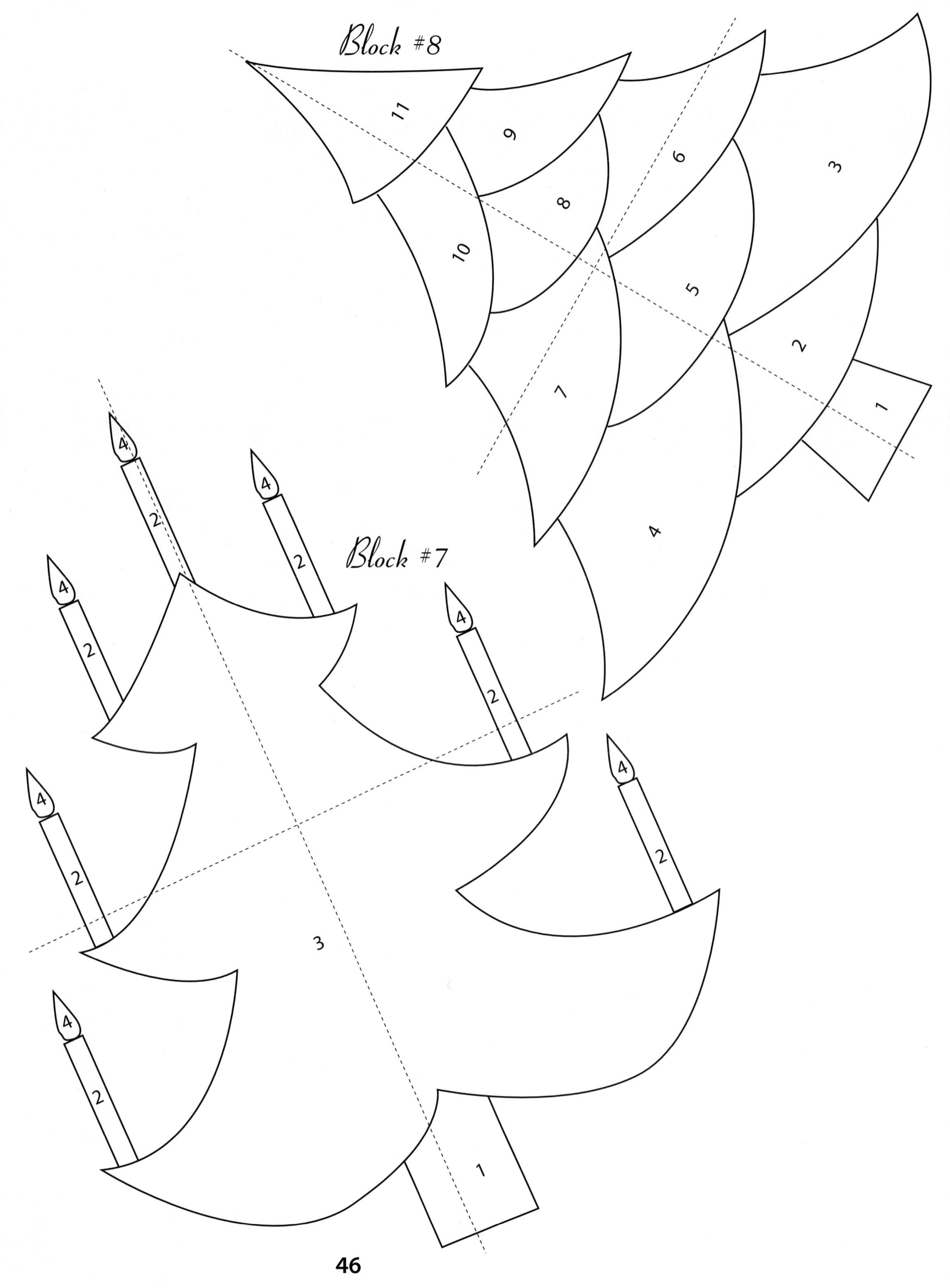

Block #8
11
10
9
8
7
6
5
4
3
2
1
Block #7
4
2
4
2
4
2
4
2
4
2
4
2
4
2
3
1

The Christmas Trees

Block #4

Block #9

Block #10

Block #12

Block #10
4
5
5
5
5
3
1
2
5
5
Embroider on
the dashed lines.
25
22
Block #9
23
19 24
21
20
14
13
18 16
15
17
11
12
7
8
2
10
9
3
4
5
6
1
49

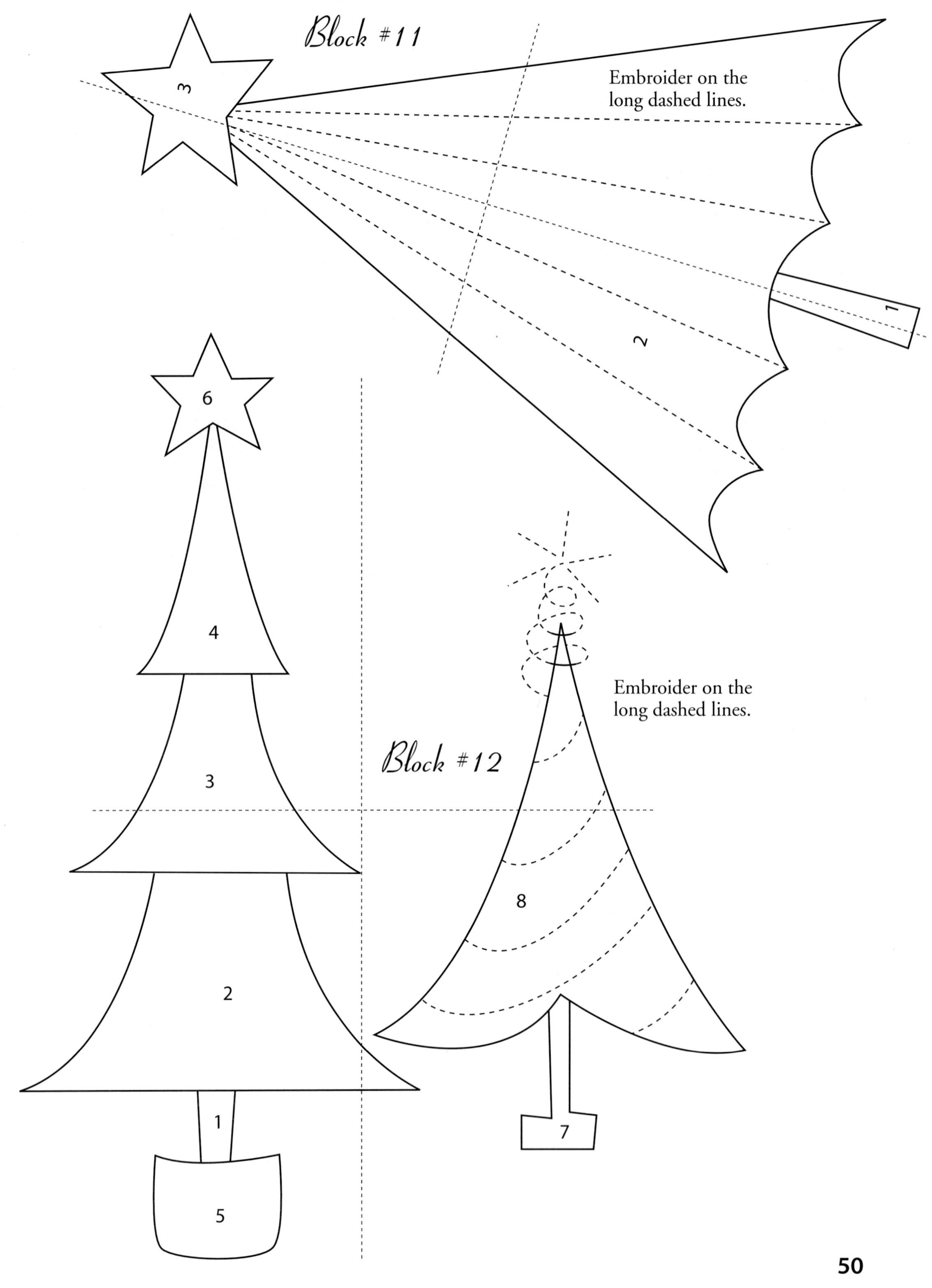

Block #11
3
Embroider on the
long dashed lines.
2
1
6
4
3
2
1
5
Block #12
Embroider on the
long dashed lines.
8
7

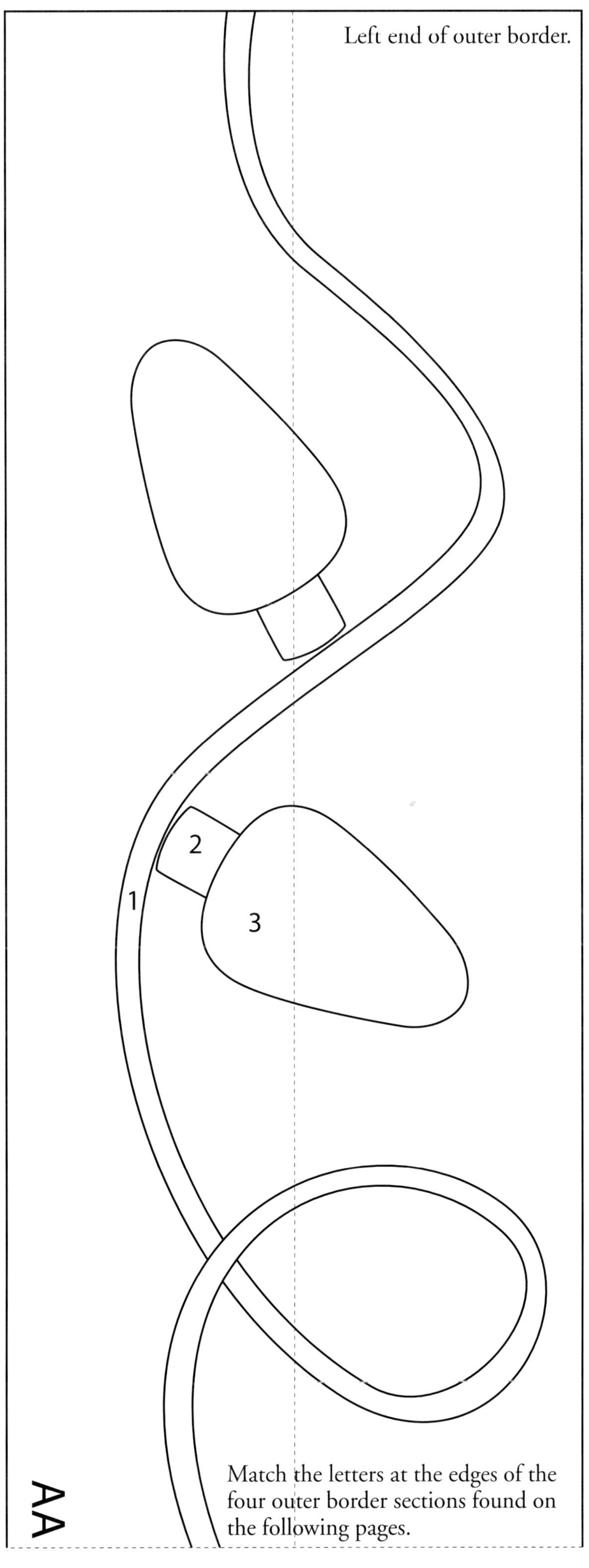

Match the letters at the edges of the
four outer border sections found on
the following pages.

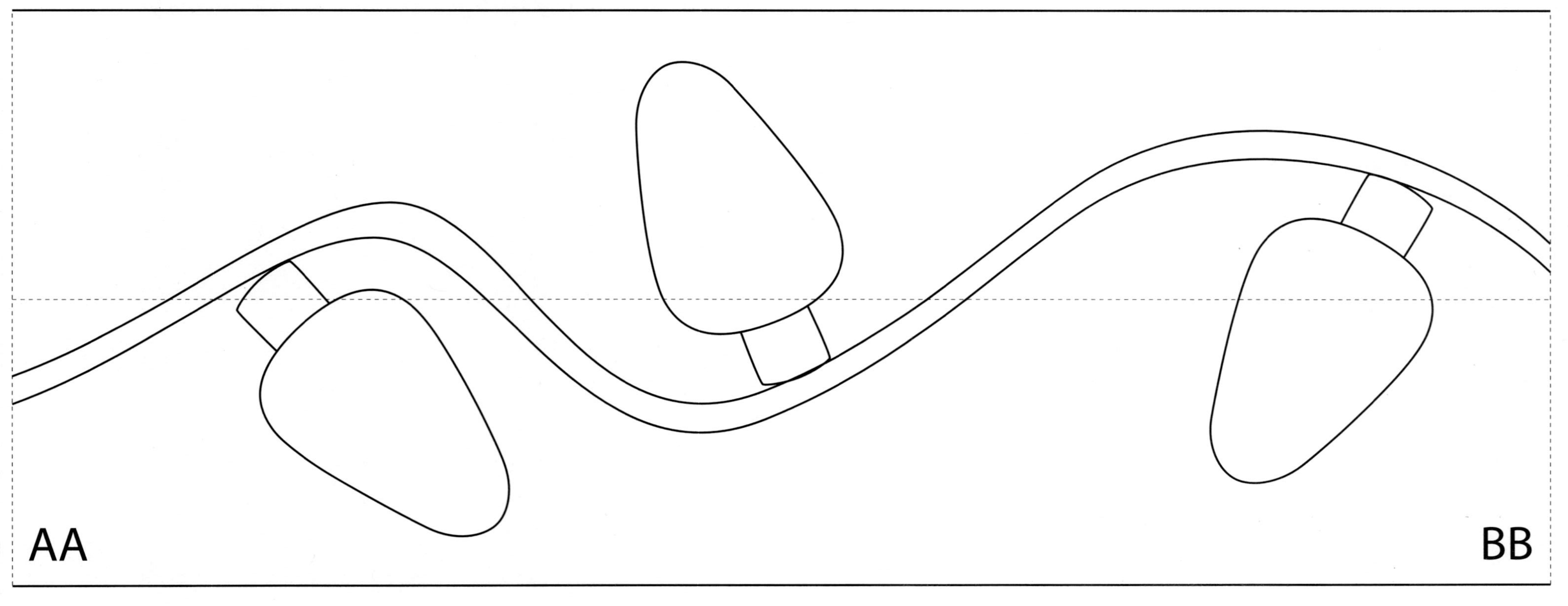

AA
BB

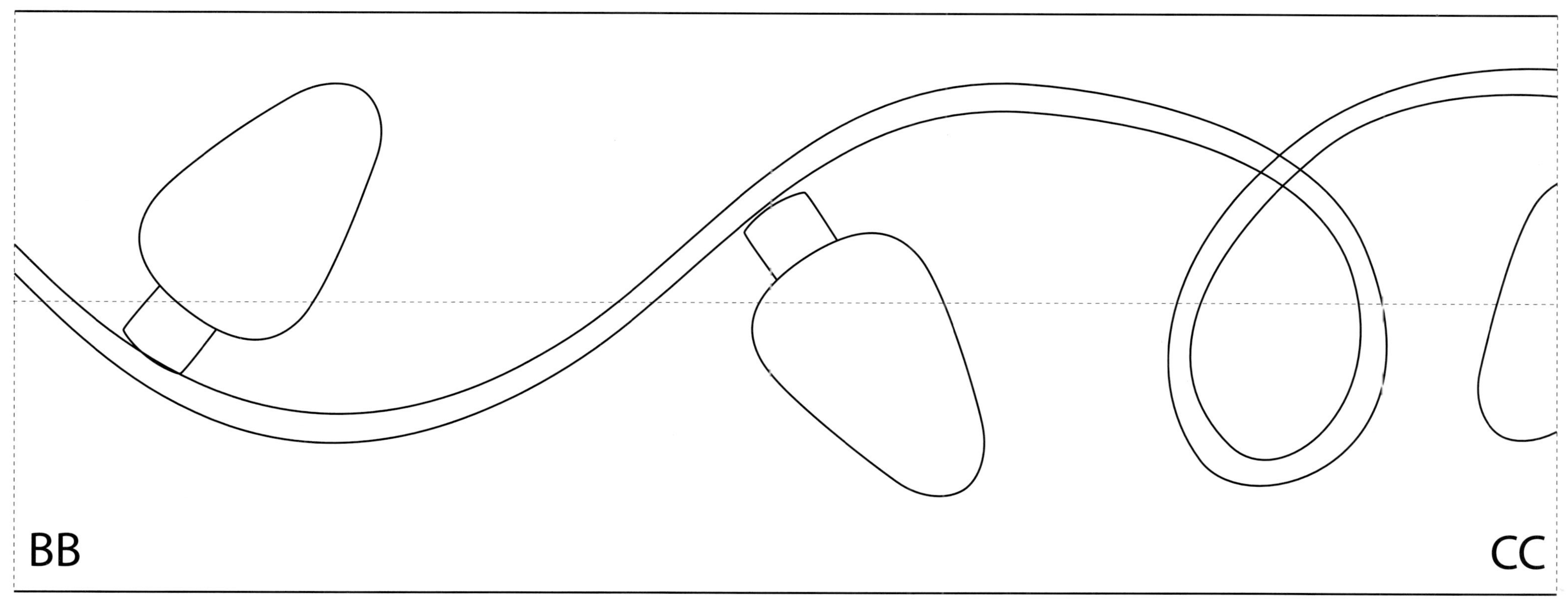

BB
CC

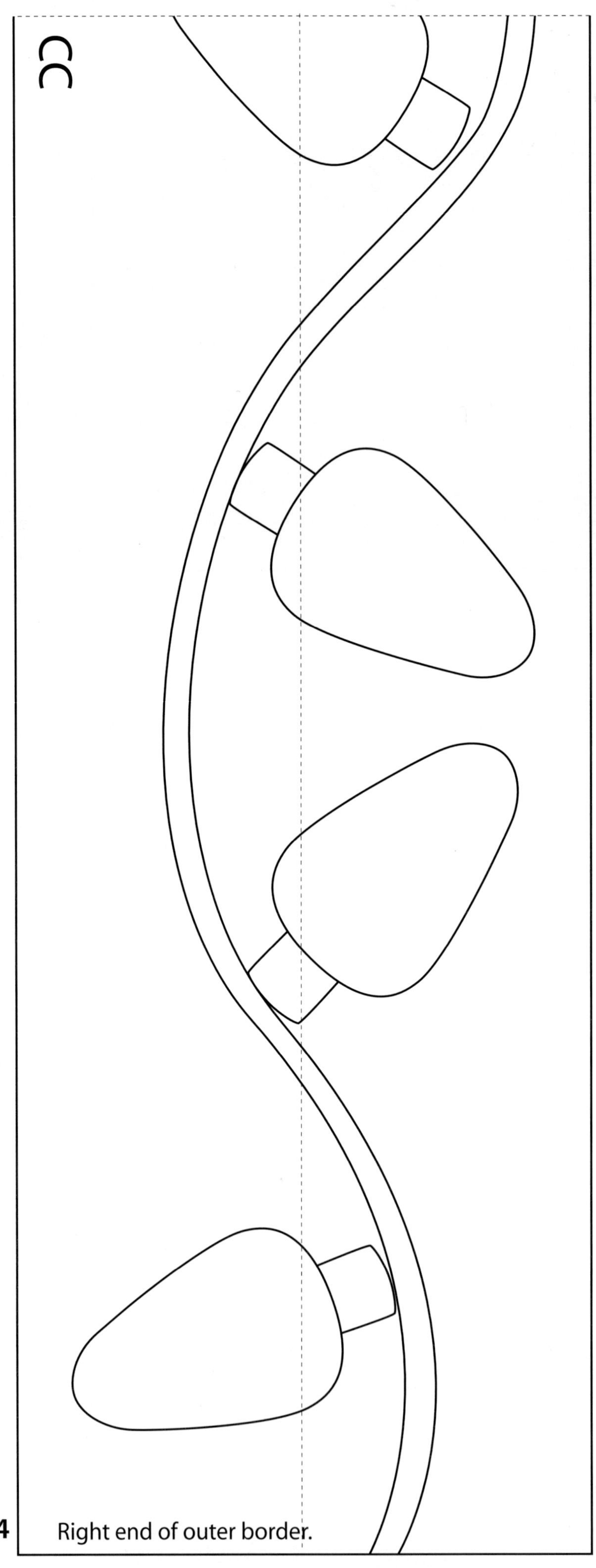

 Right end of outer border.

Christmas Trees Table Runner

FINISHED SIZE – 14" x 40"

Dress your table with this festive table runner! Begin by cutting a piece of paper 10" x 40". Use a ruler and draw a center vertical and horizontal line. Draw three gentle hills on the bottom third of one long side (see drawing above.) Choose the tree patterns for your runner and trace them in place on the paper. This paper is your pattern. Use it to make a placement overlay for the runner.

BACKGROUND – 3/8 yard
Cut one 12" x 40" strip
   Trim to 10 1/2" x 36 1/2" when your applique is complete.
INNER BORDER – 1/8 yard
Cut two strips 1" x 36 1/2"
Cut two strips 1" x 11 1/2"
OUTER BORDER – 1/4 yard
Cut two strips 2" x 37 1/2"
Cut two strips 2" x 14 1/2"
BACKING – 1/2 yard
BINDING – 5/8 yard
Make 2 1/4" continuous bias binding
NOTIONS – Sequins and beads

Assemble the Table Runner

1. Applique, press, and trim the runner block to size.
2. Sew on the top and bottom inner borders.
3. Sew on the side inner borders.
4. Sew on the top and bottom outer borders.
5. Sew on the side outer borders.
6. Layer, baste, and quilt your runner.
7. Sew on the hard embellishments.

Reindeer Playground

Yardage & Cutting

Finished size – 47" square

Background fabrics – 1 1/4 yards muslin

Cut nine 14" squares

Note: If your fabric shrinks to less than 42" wide after washing, cut 13" squares. Trim to 12 1/2" square when applique is complete.

Sashing fabric & outer border corner fabric – 1/2 yard

Cut twenty-four 1 1/2" x 12 1/2" strips

Cut four 3 1/2" squares

Sashing squares – 1/8 yard

Cut sixteen 1 1/2" squares

Inner border fabric – 1/8-1/4 yard

Note: If your fabric shrinks to less than 42" wide, you will need to piece these strips.

Cut two 1" x 40 1/2" strips (sides)

Cut two 1" x 41 1/2" strips. (top and bottom)

Outer border fabric – 1/2 yard

Note: If your fabric shrinks to less than 42" wide, you will need to piece these strips.

Cut four 3 1/2" x 41 1/2" strips

Continuous bias binding fabric – 3/4 yard

Make 2 1/2" wide continuous bias binding.

Backing and sleeve fabric – 3 1/8 yards

Notions – Red sequins and beads

Assemble the Quilt

1. Applique the nine reindeer blocks.
2. Embroider the reindeer names.
3. Press and trim the blocks to size.
4. Set the blocks, sashing strips, and sashing corners together as shown at right.
5. Sew on the side inner borders.
6. Sew on the top and bottom inner borders.
7. Sew on the side borders.
8. Sew an outer border corner square to each end of the top and bottom outer borders. Sew these borders to the quilt.
9. Layer, baste and quilt the quilt.
10. Sew on the sequin berries.
11. Make and attach the sleeve and documentation patch (page 11).

Special Instructions for the Reindeer Eyes

Trace around the reindeer template onto the reindeer fabric. Lay the reindeer fabric over the reindeer pattern, lining up the tracing on the fabric with the pattern. Use permanent gel or paint pens and trace the eyes. You may have to go over the white areas more than once.

If you cannot see through your fabric try freehanding the eyes onto the fabric. Practice on paper first. The eyes are bean shaped – it helps to draw the "bean" first and then fill in the details.

The Reindeer Blocks

The blocks are numbered from left to right, top to bottom. For example, Block #1 is located in the upper left hand corner of the quilt.

The berries on each reindeer's neck are sequins secured with a tiny bead.

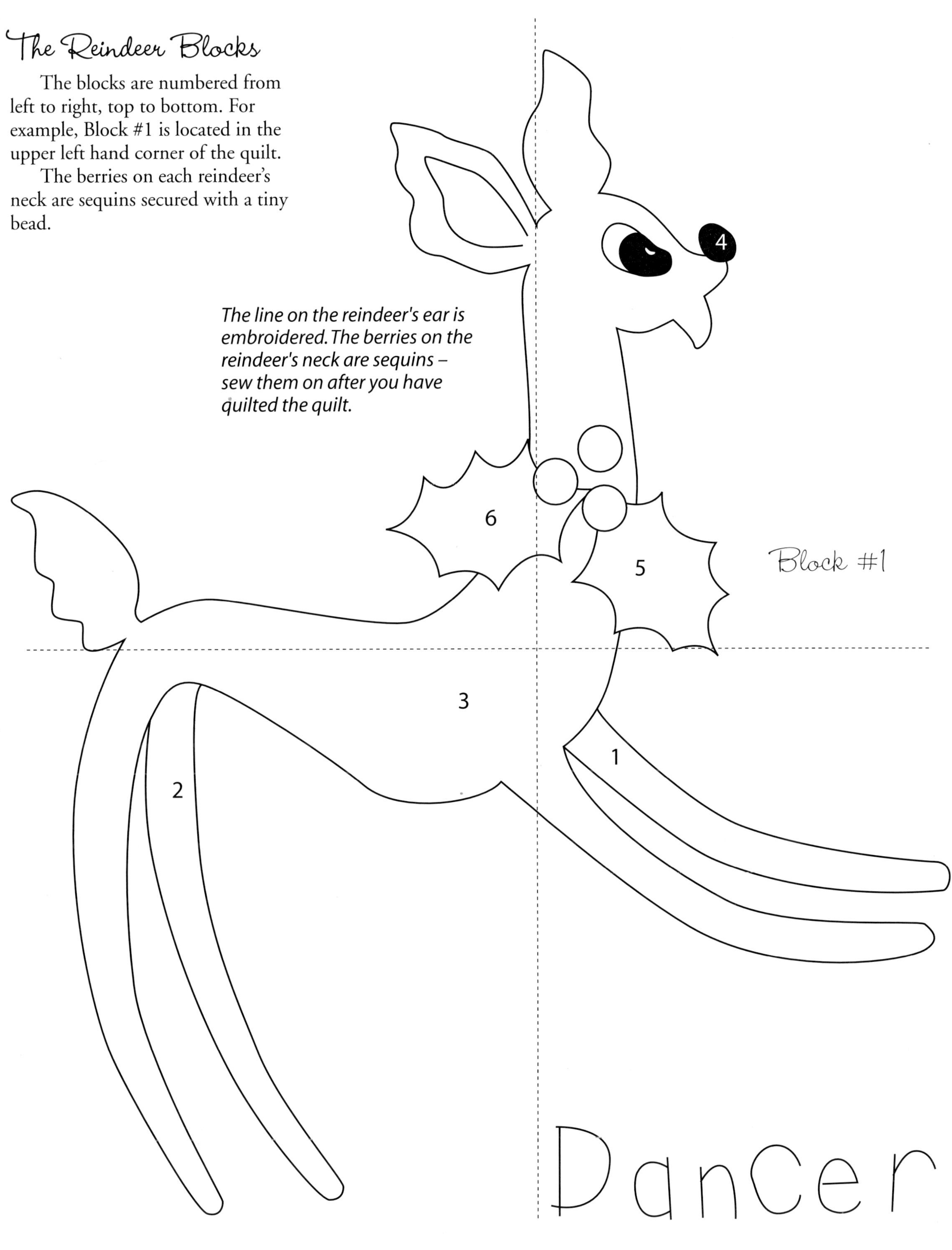

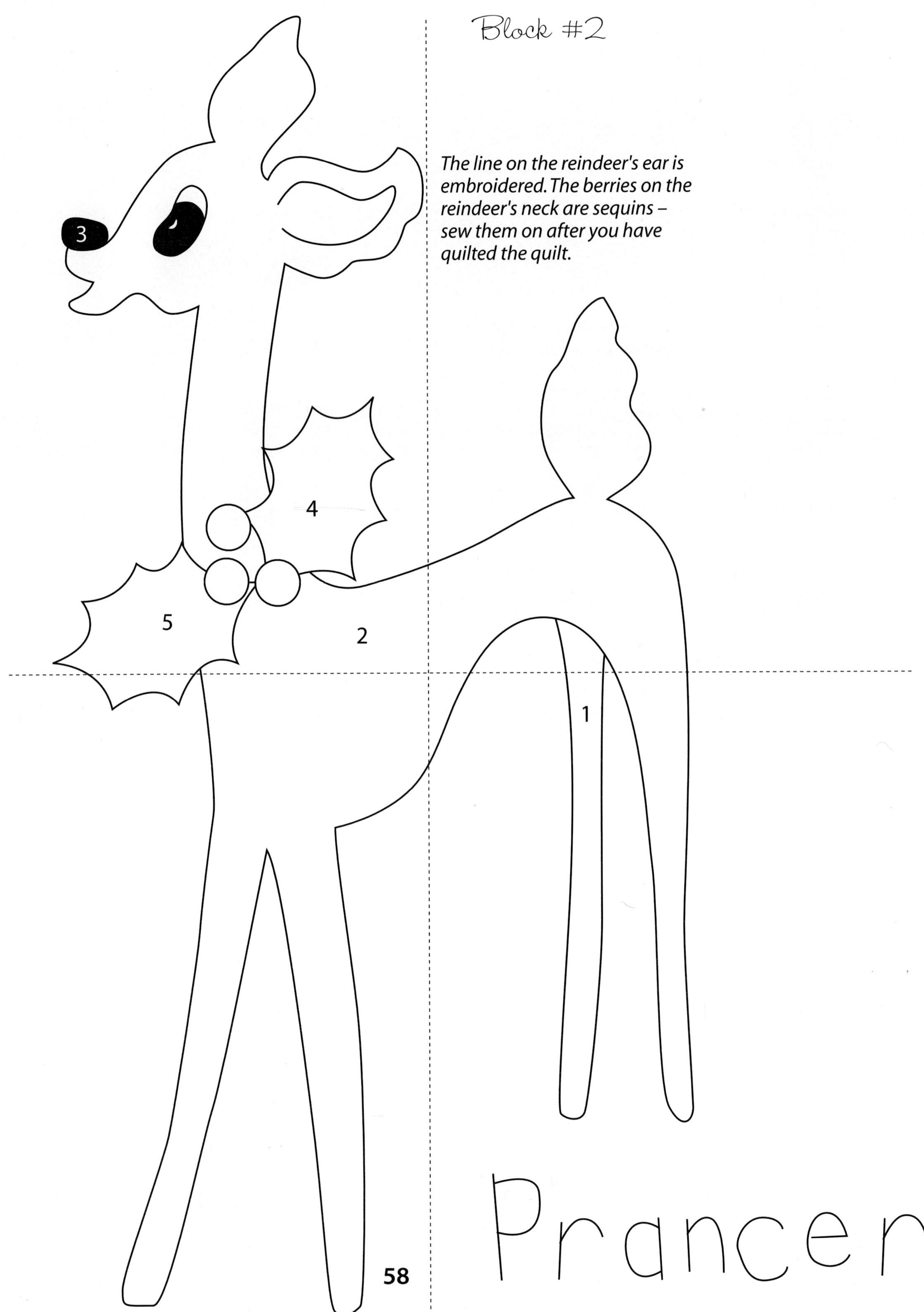
Block #2
The line on the reindeer's ear is embroidered. The berries on the reindeer's neck are sequins – sew them on after you have quilted the quilt.
3
4
5
2
1
58
Prancer

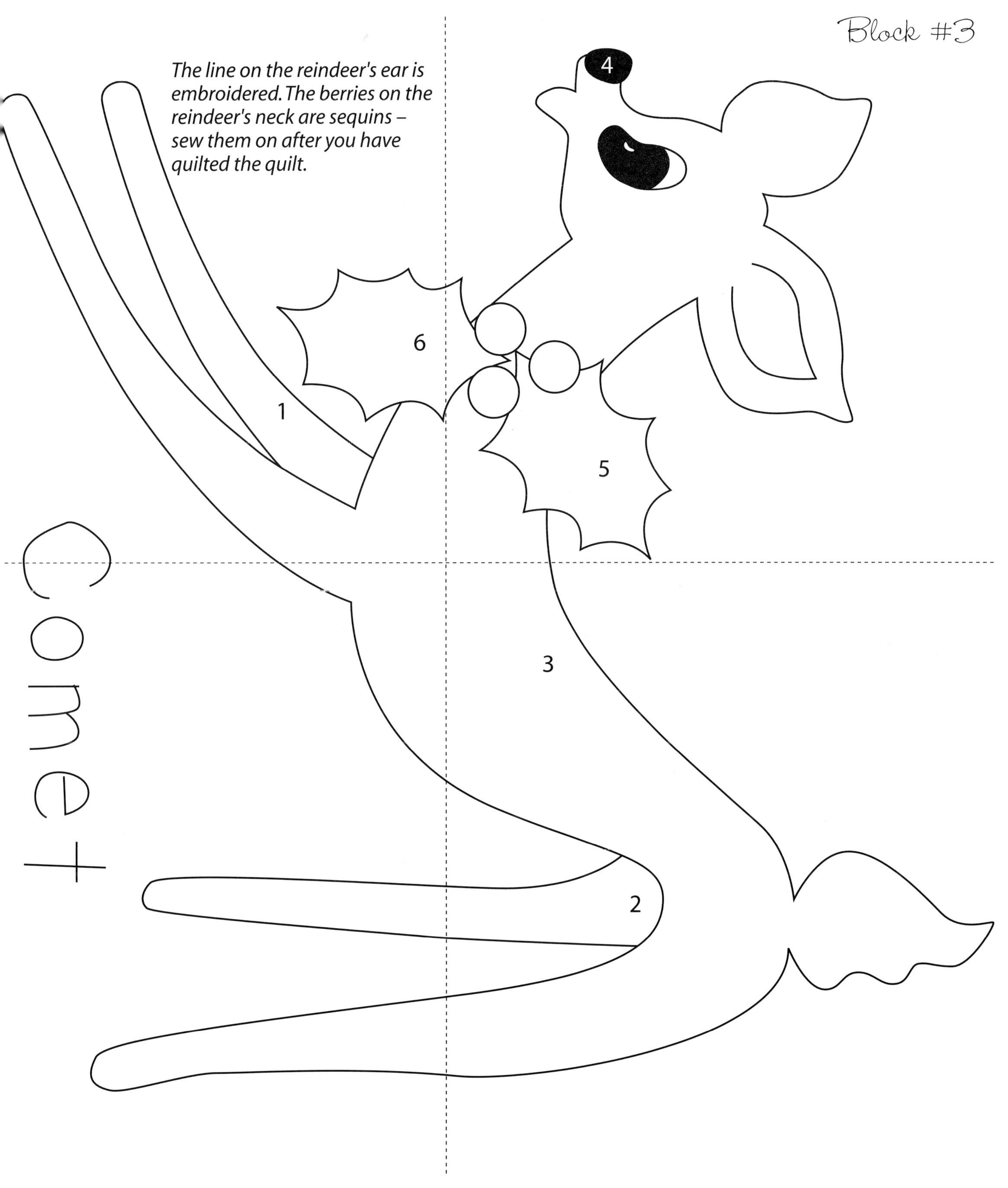
The line on the reindeer's ear is
embroidered. The berries on the
reindeer's neck are sequins –
sew them on after you have
quilted the quilt.
6
1
4
5
3
2
Comet

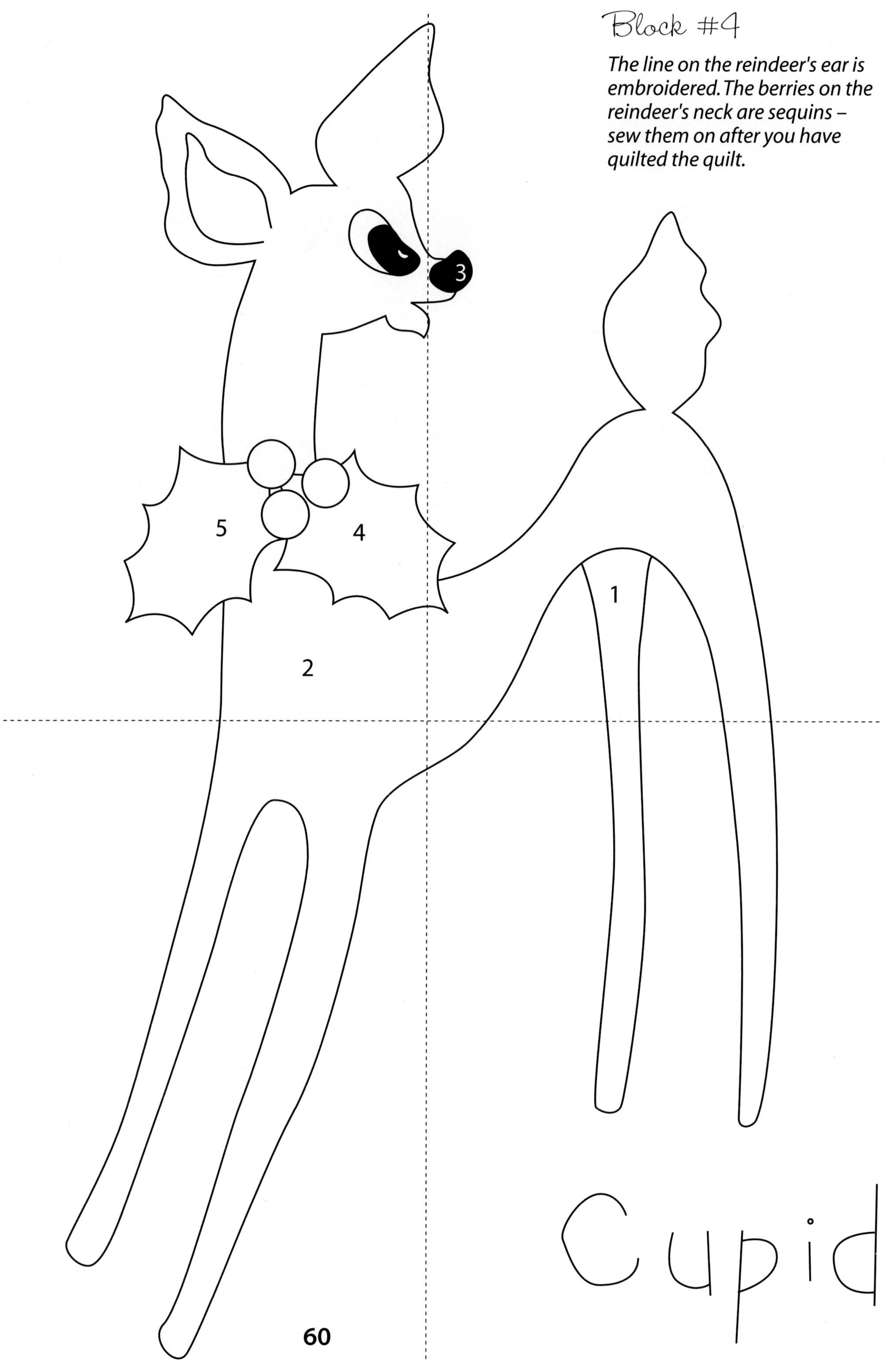

Block #4

The line on the reindeer's ear is
embroidered. The berries on the
reindeer's neck are sequins –
sew them on after you have
quilted the quilt.

3
5
4
1
2

Cupid

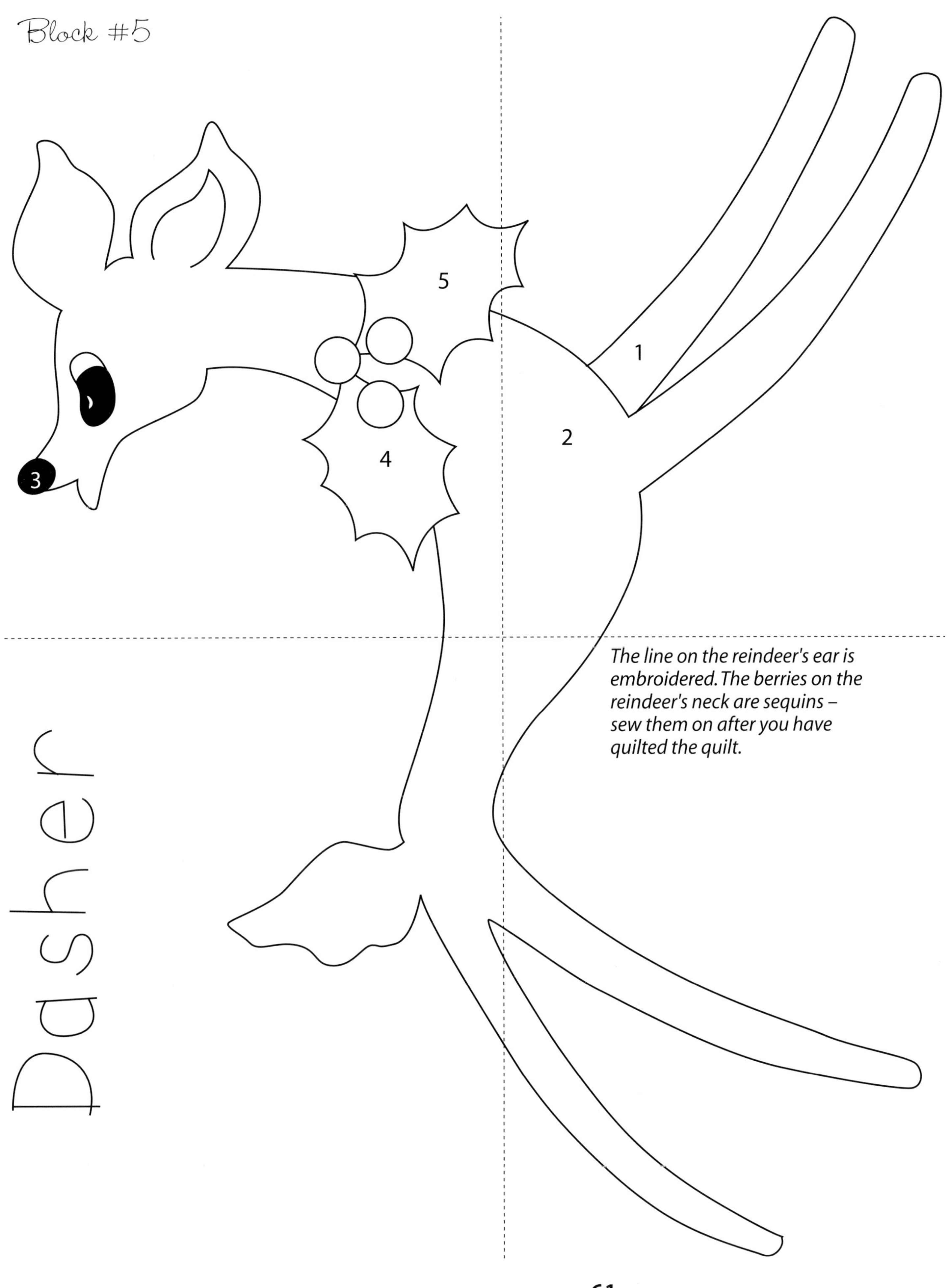

Dasher
5
1
2
3
4
The line on the reindeer's ear is
embroidered. The berries on the
reindeer's neck are sequins –
sew them on after you have
quilted the quilt.

Donner

The line on the reindeer's ear is embroidered. The berries on the reindeer's neck are sequins – sew them on after you have quilted the quilt.

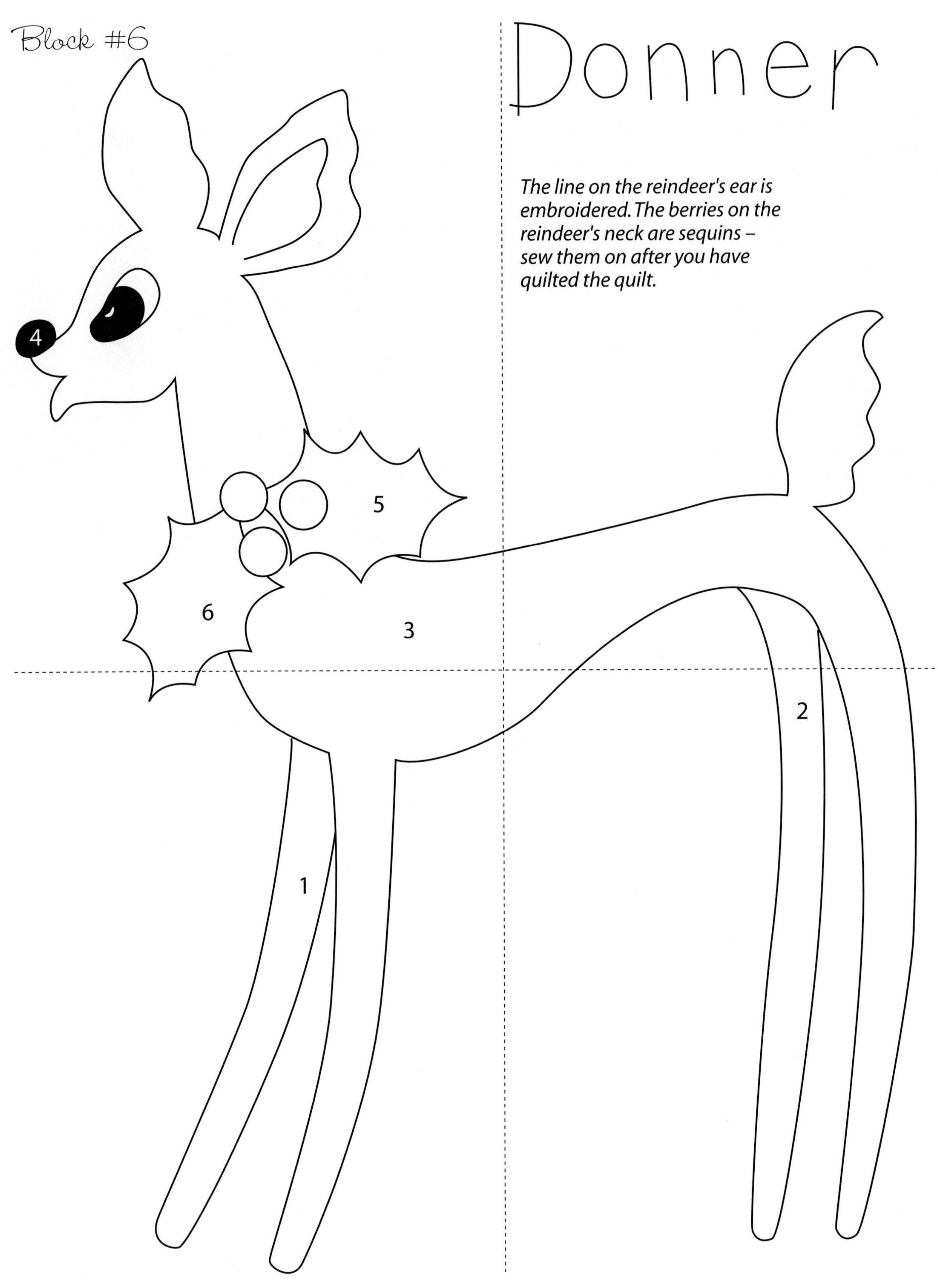

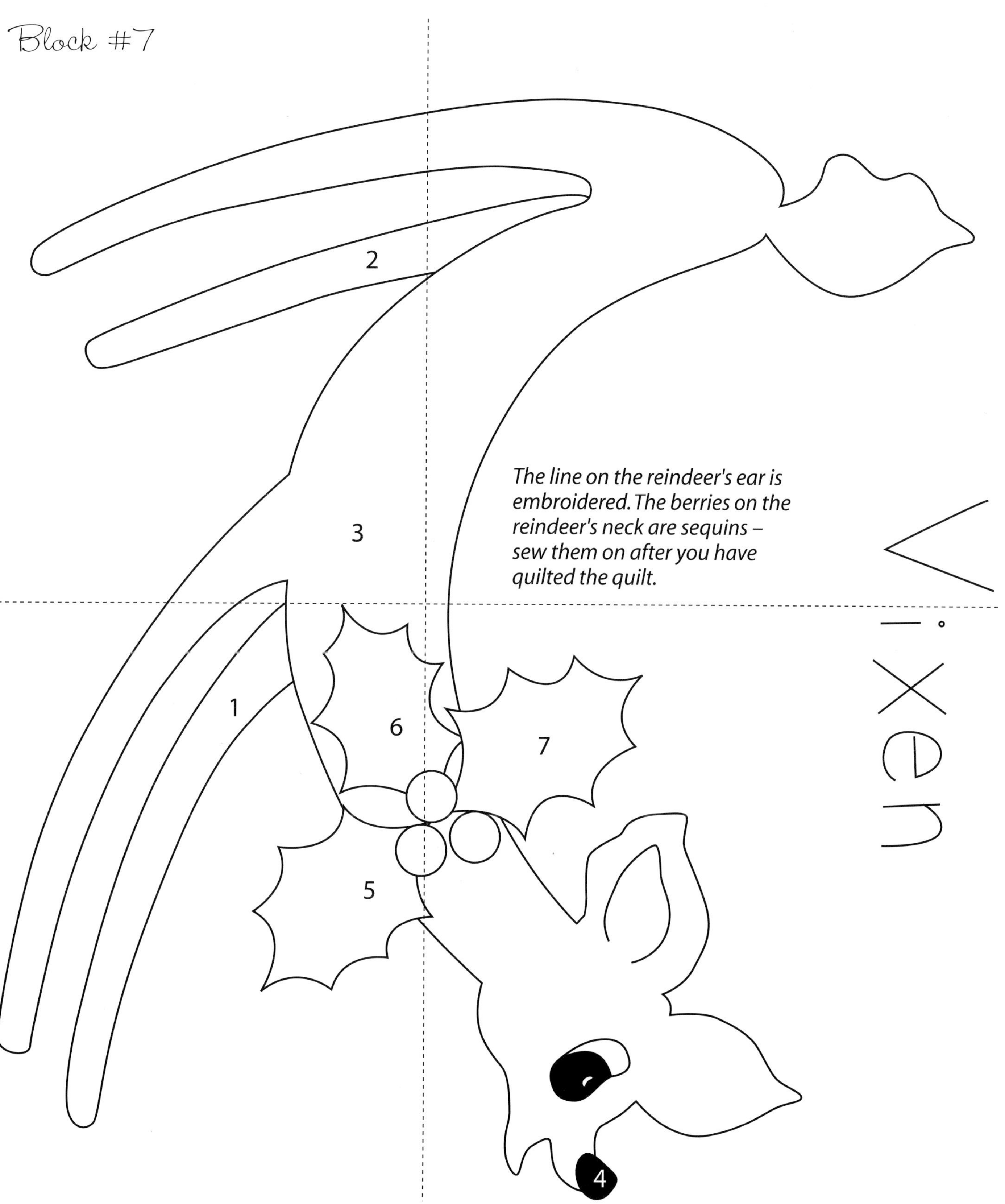
2
63
3
1
6
7
5
4
V i x e n
The line on the reindeer's ear is
embroidered. The berries on the
reindeer's neck are sequins –
sew them on after you have
quilted the quilt.

Block #8

The line on the reindeer's ear is embroidered. The berries on the reindeer's neck are sequins – sew them on after you have quilted the quilt.

Blitzen

3
6
5
4
2
1

Reindeer Playground

Blitzen

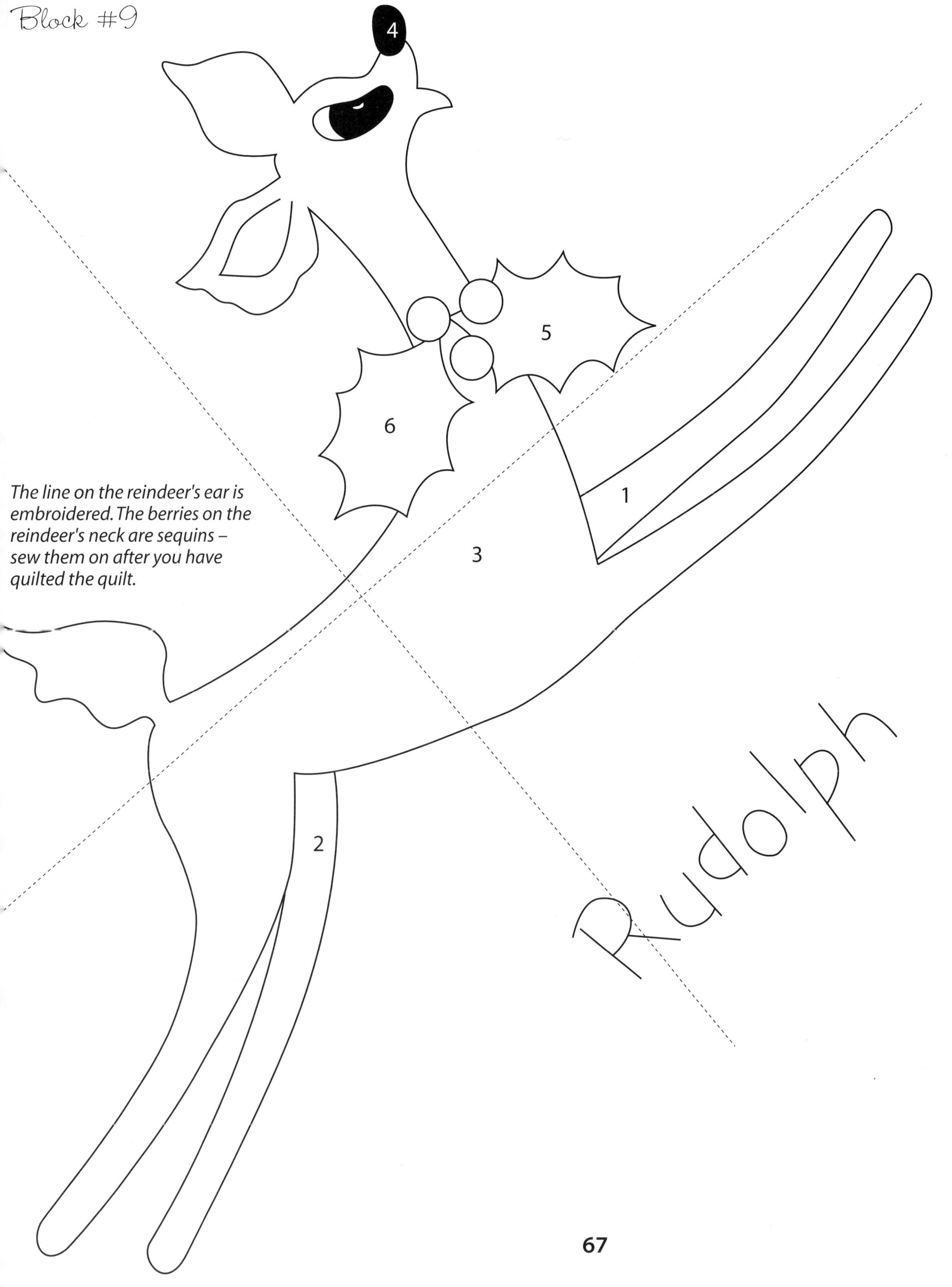

The line on the reindeer's ear is embroidered. The berries on the reindeer's neck are sequins – sew them on after you have quilted the quilt.

Techniques

Cutaway Applique

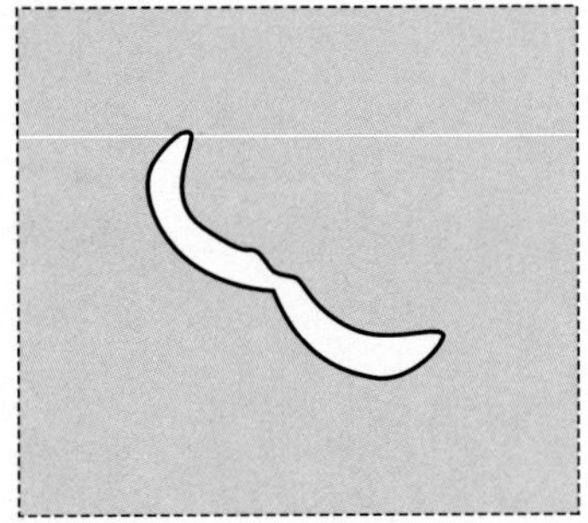

1. Place the mustache template on top of the mustache fabric, both right sides up. Be sure to lay the template on the fabric so that most of the edges will be on the diagonal grain of the fabric. Trace the mustache.

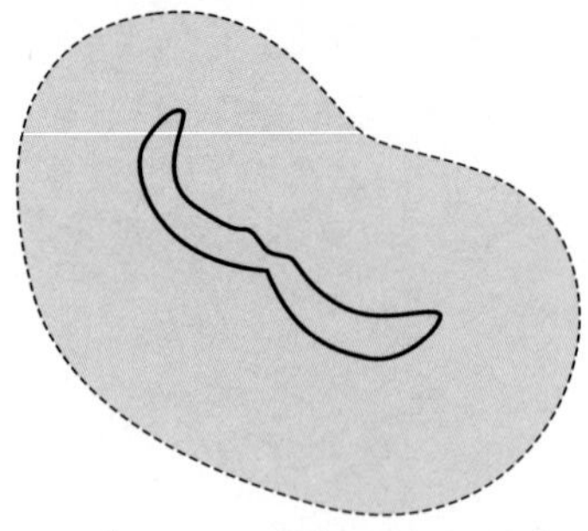

2. Cut the mustache out of the piece of mustache fabric. Leave 1" or more of excess fabric around the mustache. Finger press the drawn line under.

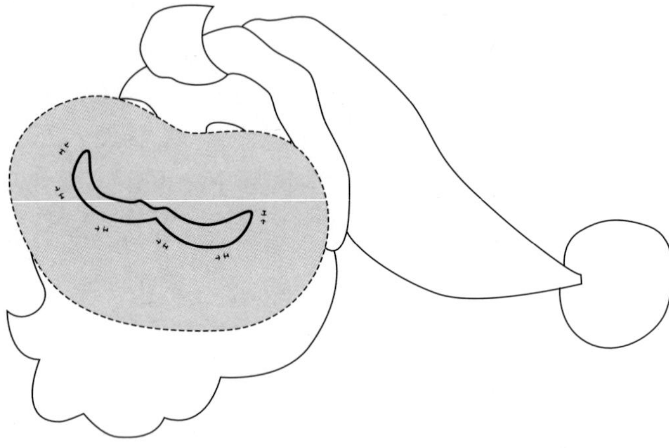

3. Use your overlay to position the mustache onto your block. Pin it in place. Position the pins on the outside edge of the mustache. In cutaway applique, always sew the concave side first.

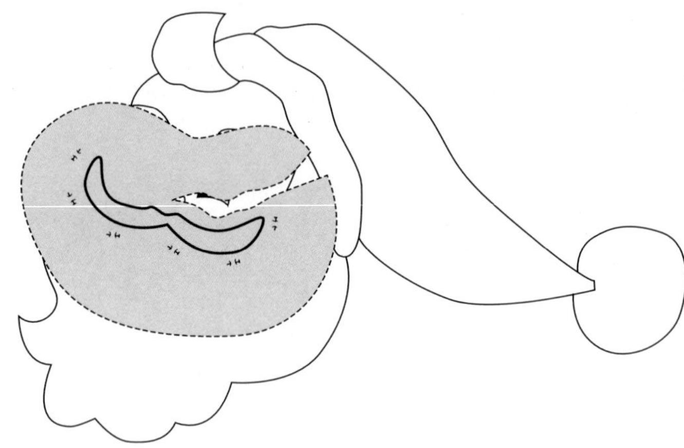

4. Begin cutting away the excess fabric, leaving a 3/16" or smaller seam allowance. Stitch the concave side first.

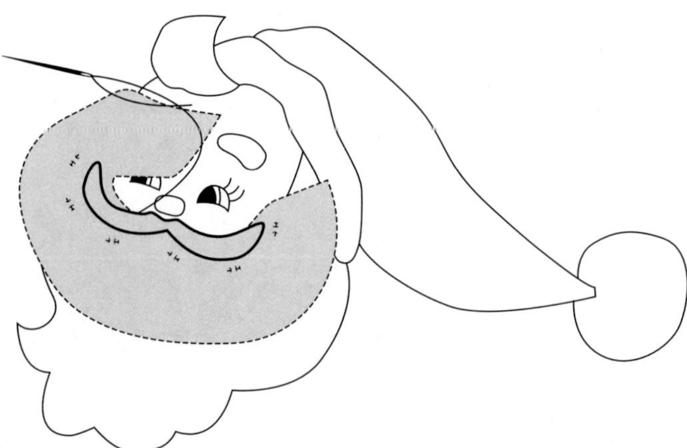

5. The mustache is being stitched. More fabric is trimmed away as you go. Clip inner points when you can no longer turn the seam allowance under nicely.

6. Remove the pins as you stitch the second side of the mustache. Clip away excess fabric as necessary.

Circles

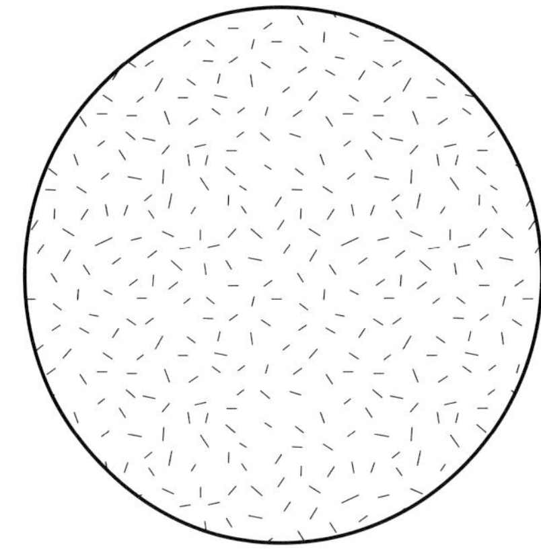

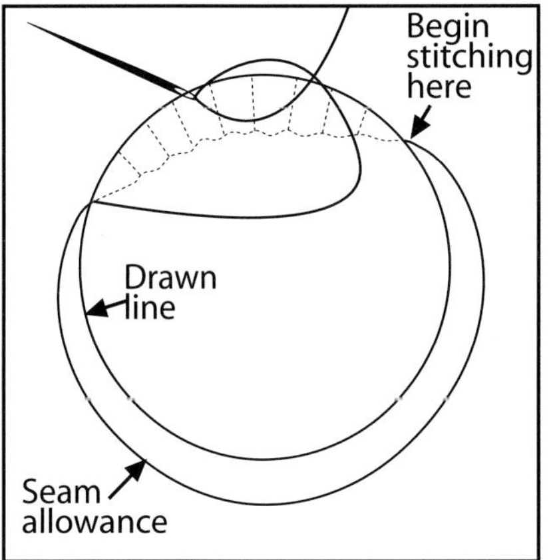

1. Finger press all circles before you pin
   them in place. Begin sewing. Control
   the edge one stitch at a time.

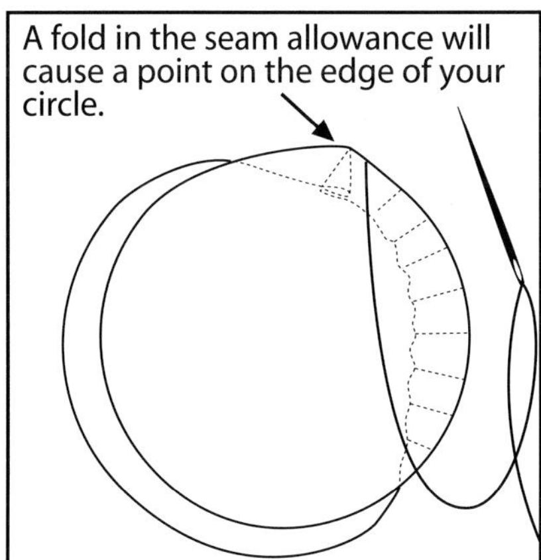

2. As you turn under a curve the seam
   allowance can fold over itself and
   cause a point in the outer edge.

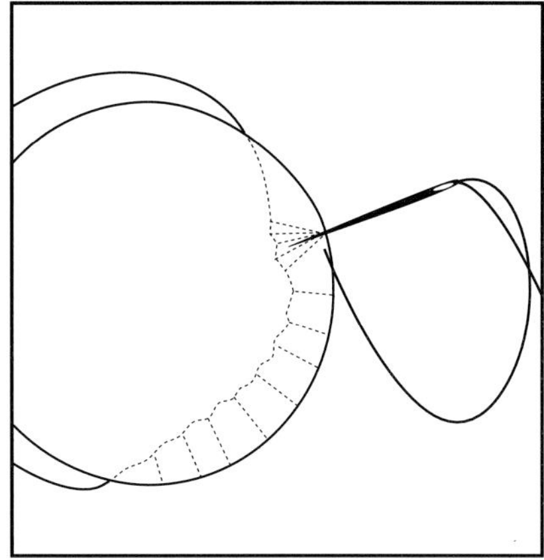

3. Reach in with the tip of your needle
   and open up the fold. Smooth the
   curve and stitch.

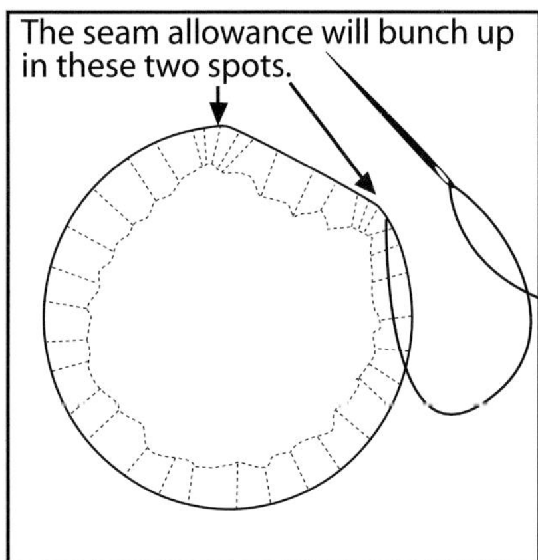

4. The last 1/4"-3/8" of the circle will
   want to turn under all at once.
   When you turn it under this part of
   the circle will flatten out.

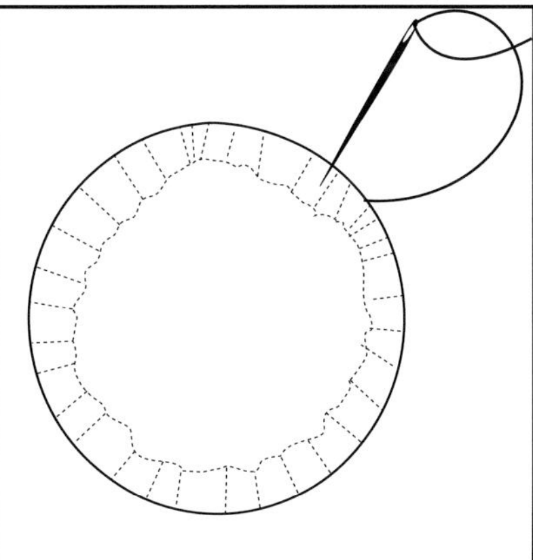

5. Use the tip of your needle to smooth
   out the bunched seam allowance and
   to pull the flattened part of the circle
   into a more round shape.

Use reverse applique any time you want to cut through one piece of fabric to reveal the fabric below it.

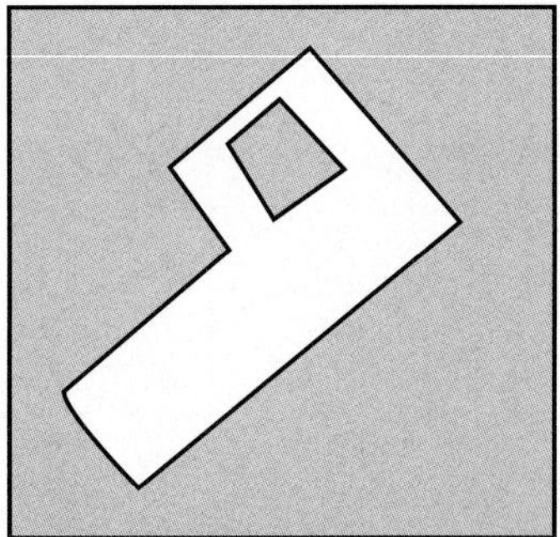

1. Place the train caboose template on top of the train caboose fabric, both right sides up. Be sure to lay the template on the fabric so that most of the edges will be on the diagonal grain of the fabric. Trace the caboose.

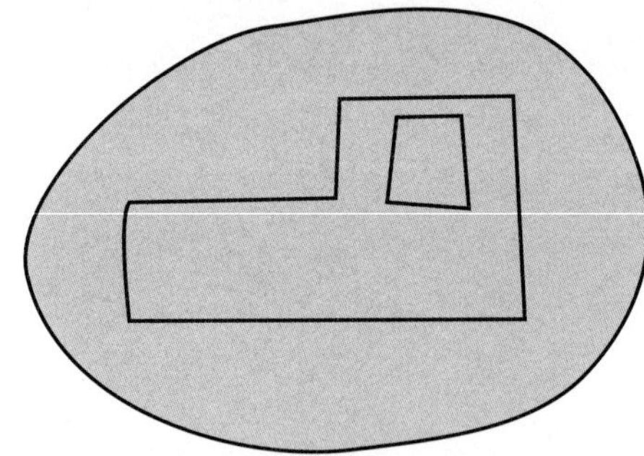

2. Cut out the caboose. Leave 1" or more of excess fabric around it. Finger press the drawn line of the window.

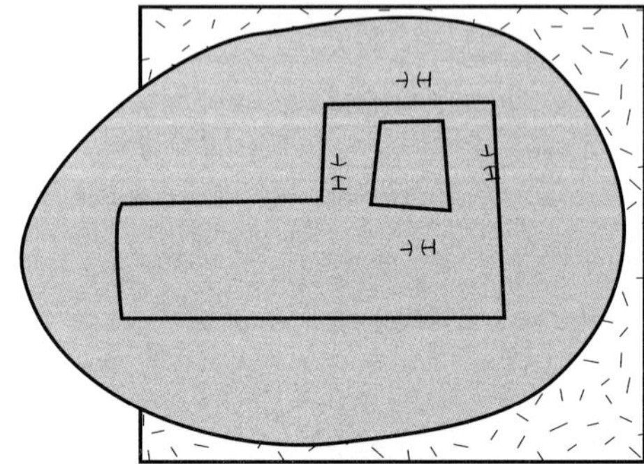

3. Pin the caboose fabric to a piece of fabric that will be the inside of the window.

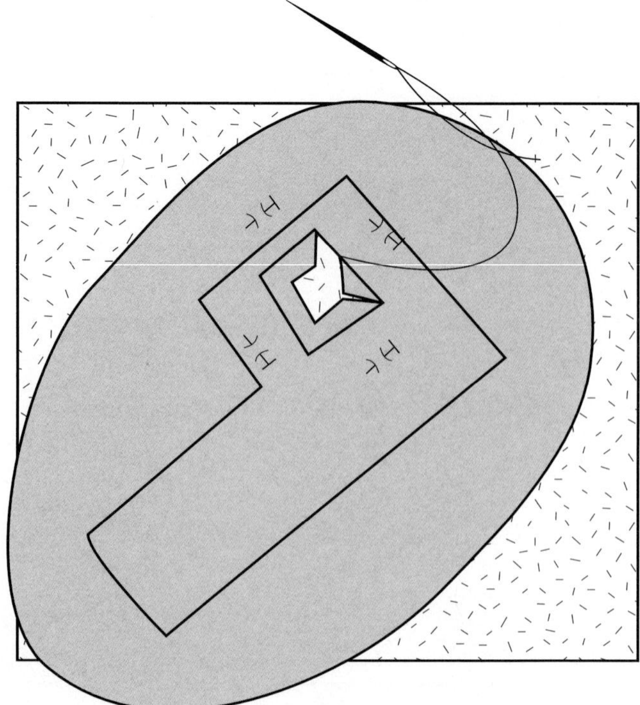

4. Cut away the excess fabric from the center of the window leaving a scant seam allowance. Clip two corners and begin sewing the seam allowance under between the clips. Never begin sewing at a point.

5. Finish sewing the window. Turn the unit over and cut away the excess window fabric, leaving a seam allowance. From the right side, cut out the caboose unit, leaving a 3/16" seam allowance. Sew the caboose unit in place on your block.

Making Continuous Bias

1. Start with a square of fabric.

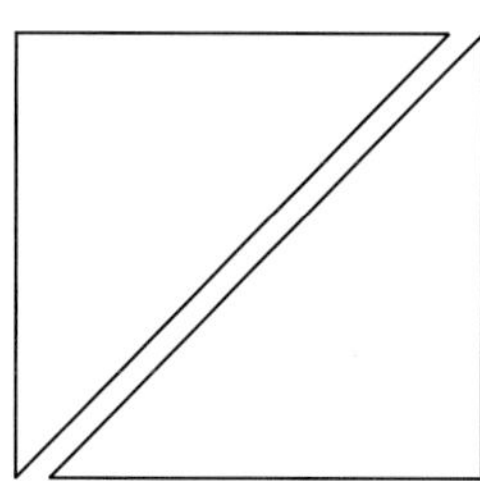

2. Cut it in half diagonally.

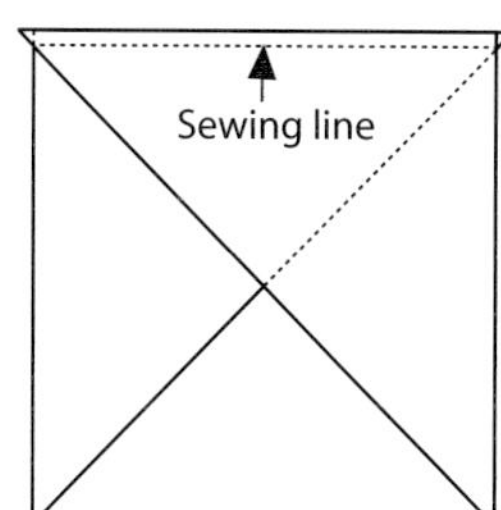

3. Sew the two triangles together, right sides together, as shown. You are always sewing together fabric that is on the straight of grain.

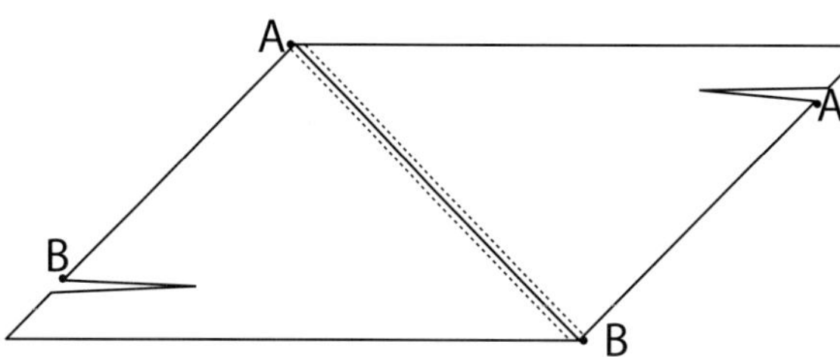

4. Press seam allowances open.

   If you are making bias for stems, press the seams to one side.

   Cut the strip the width you want your bias strip to be.

   Cut into each side about 4" as shown.

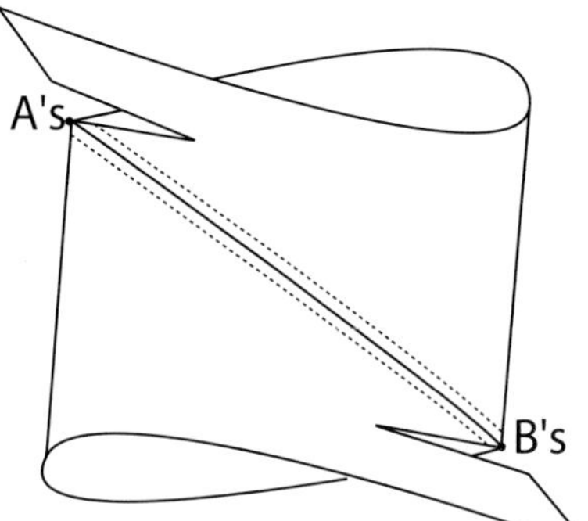

5. Match the A's and B's with the fabric right sides together. Sew and press seam open.

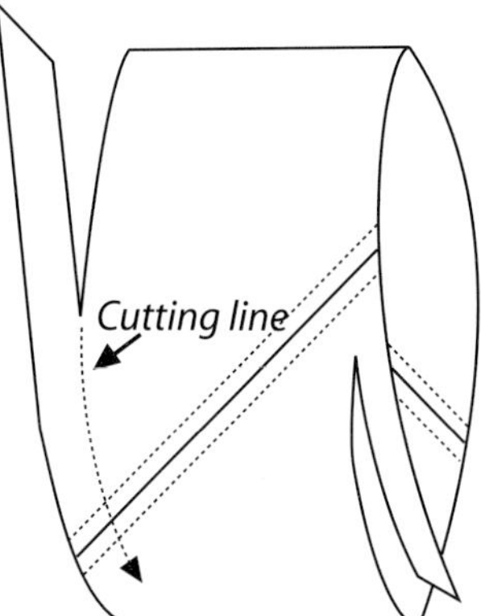

6. Using your rotary cutter and ruler, cut your continuous bias strip.

Sewing Binding to the Quilt

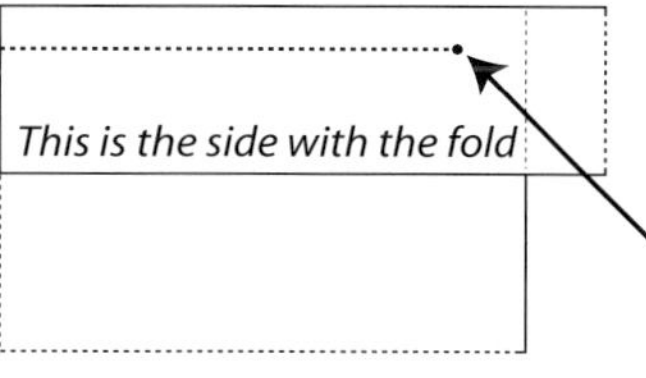

1. Press your continuous bias strip in half lengthwise, wrong sides together. Leave 6" of the binding unsewn above where you start sewing. You will need this unsewn end later. Begin sewing binding to the quilt top with a 1/4" seam allowance. Match the raw edges of the binding with the right side, raw edges of the quilt.

   At the corner, stop sewing 1/4" away from the edge of the quilt.

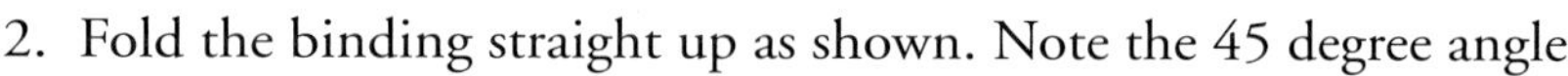

2. Fold the binding straight up as shown. Note the 45 degree angle.

3. Fold the binding straight down and begin sewing the next side of the quilt here.

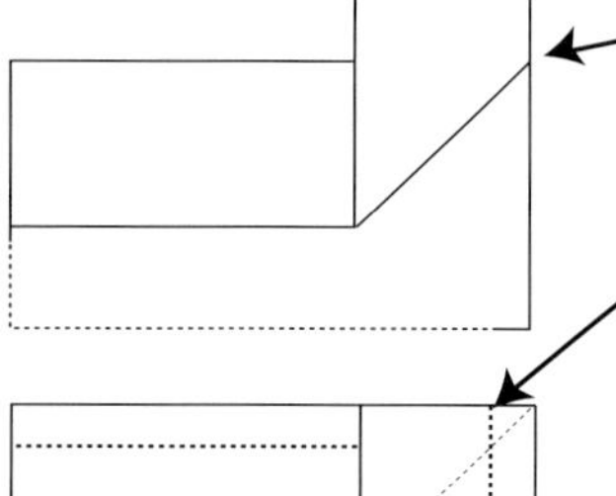

5. Sew the binding to all sides of the quilt. When you get back to where you started, carefully cut off the excess binding – make sure that you leave a seam allowance! Sew the ends of the binding together and finish sewing the binding to the quilt top.

6. Turn the binding to the back of the quilt, covering all raw edges.
   Hand stitch the folded edge of the binding to the back of the quilt.

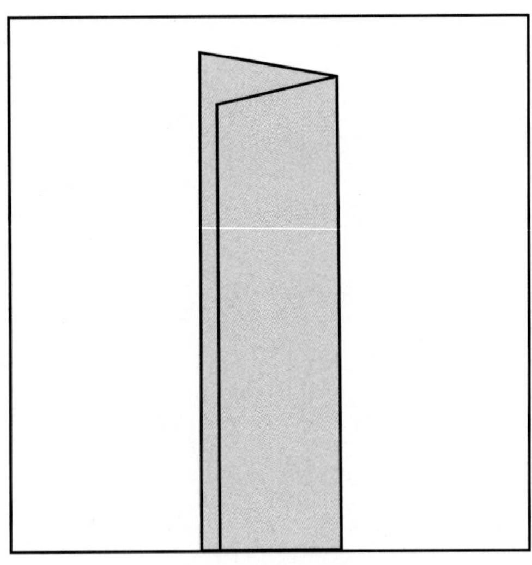

1. Make a continuous strip (see previous page) 11/2" wide. Press in half, right sides out.

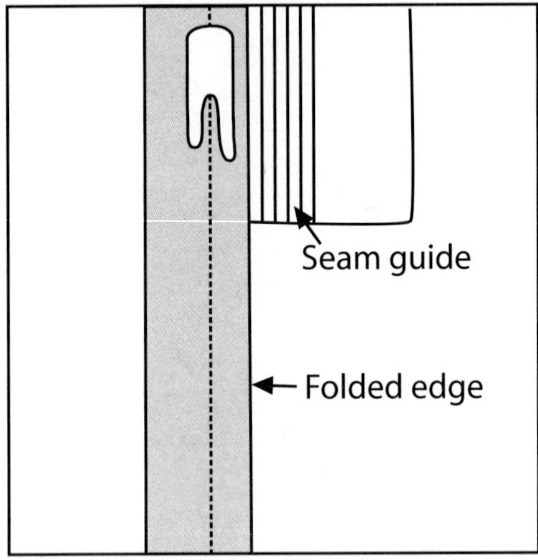

2. Place the folded edge of the bias strip against the seam guide of your sewing machine and sew.

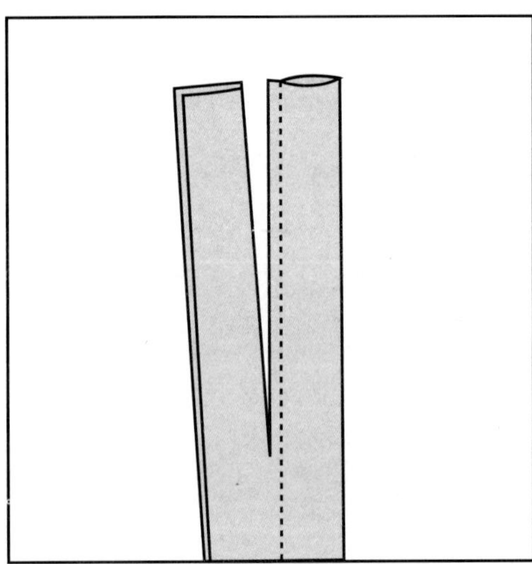

3. Trim away excess fabric, leaving a very scant seam allowance.

Bias Stem

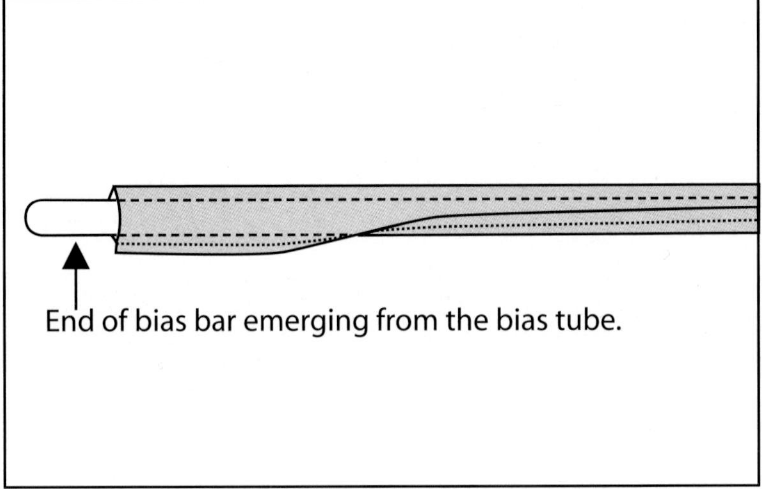

4. Insert the 1/4" bias bar into your sewn bias tube. Shift the seam and seam allowance to the back of the bar and press it in place. Remove the bias bar.

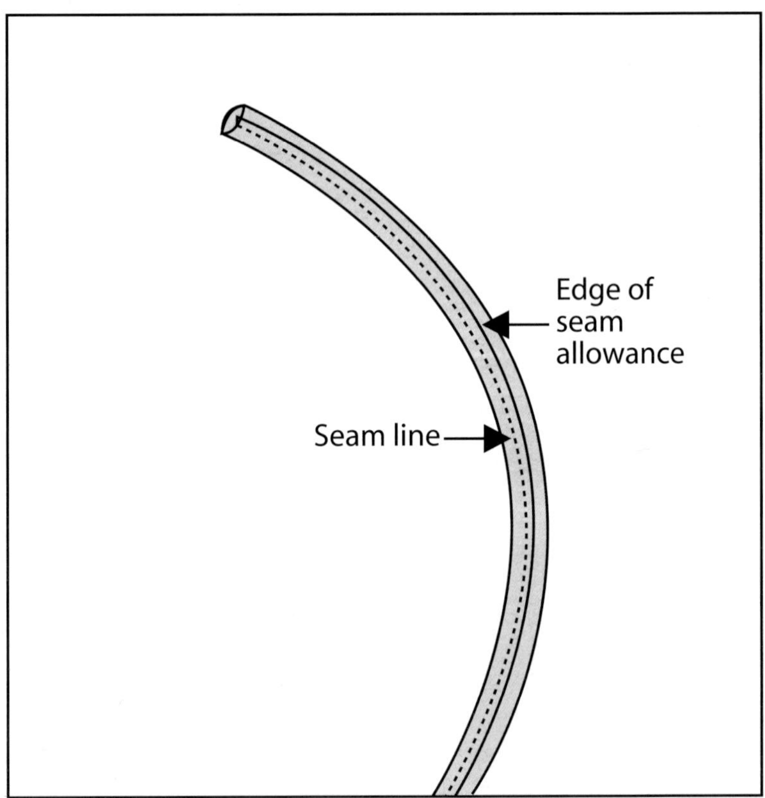

5. Hold up the finished bias stem. You'll notice that it wants to curve better in one direction than the other. The side closest to the seam line makes the tighter curve. When possible, match this side of the bias stem to the concave side of the stem on your pattern.